ENDORSEMENTS

"For years I have been blessed by the preaching and Bible teaching of Bert Jones. Now, you can be too. With his *Dig In!* devotional outlines, Bert leads us to scriptural insights pertinent to the spiritual questions we encounter throughout our lives. The format is a guide, inviting our participation. The results of this journey will be a greater understanding of God and His Word, as well as how they can shape our lives. My recommendation...*Dig In!*"

GENE RUDD, MD
Christian Medical & Dental Associations

"What a wonderful gift to my life this book is! *Dig In!* gives me a front row seat and a way to learn on my own from sermons I didn't get to hear delivered in person. Bert Jones has a wonderful way of distilling and compacting the ordered and arranged truths of God. That gift makes 'digging in' to God's Word a delight. As you read and invest your time in these pages, you will see scholarship in hermeneutics and excellence in expository preaching. I've been a pastor for 56 years. I know what the words, the spirit-driven ideas and the outlines in this book represent. The *actual* cost for these pages FAR exceeds the purchase price of the book. You will see the heart and mind and passion of a wonderful pastor. However, no one but Jesus and Bert know how many lonely Saturday nights he spent crafting these thoughts for Sunday mornings, praying over these ideas for Bible studies and, especially, wrestling with the self-doubts the enemy notoriously brings to pastors as they prepare. I get to enjoy the fruit of Bert's labor of love over his many years of study and scholarship, now. Thank you, Bert, for this wonderful and exceedingly expensive gift, *Dig In!*. I consider it, truly, the gift of a lifetime."

KEN JONES
Certified Physician Life Development Coach
Pastor, Author of If I Should Die Before I Live

"Bert Jones not only inspires, but he also equips you with truths from God's Word that elevate your mind and your spirit. *Dig In!* helps you gain knowledge and encouragement that will draw you closer to the Lord while empowering you to serve in His kingdom. This daily devotional proves that the deeper you dig, the more you'll grow in your walk with Christ."

STEVE SCHELLIN
Pastor, Southland Community Church, Greenwood, Indiana

"Bert Jones has provided a resource for personal study that I have always wanted to find. His book becomes a personal guide to dig deeper for myself into God's Word on a daily basis. His 35 years of biblical study and preaching creates a wonderful template for a believer to understand and apply God's Word into their own lives. I am confident the Holy Spirit will use this book to take you deeper in your walk of faith."

PASTOR PHIL WHETSTONE
Senior Pastor, Colonial Woods Missionary Church, Port Huron, Michigan

"In a world where spiritual growth materials can feel fragmented, Bert Jones' latest offering, *Dig In!*, stands as a remarkable resource that seamlessly weaves together Bible study, sermon preparation and personal devotion. This book is a treasure trove for healthcare professionals, pastors, teachers and laypeople alike, offering opportunity and tools that breathe life into Scripture. Anyone who needs or wants to prepare a talk, sermon or lesson from Scripture will benefit from Bert's book. Each day of the year, readers are provided with themed Scripture prompts that invite deeper consideration of the subject and a solid framework for crafting impactful sermons or meaningful devotional talks. *Dig In!* also encourages readers to reflect personally, making it a perfect companion for daily meditation and prayer. With its useful lists and thoughtful prompts, *Dig In!* will not only enhance your study and preparation but also enrich your spiritual journey. I wholeheartedly recommend it to anyone seeking to deepen their faith and communicate God's message more effectively."

RON HOUP
President and CEO, GO InterNational, Wilmore, Kentucky

"Mornings can be tough, but a daily devotional prime from Bert will encourage you to *Dig In!* to the Scriptures for yourself and come out on the other side wanting to know Christ more intimately. I am confident you will be inspired and motivated to explore the Word daily as you benefit from Bert's wisdom and passion of pursuing God's heart over the decades. He has a very special ability to break down the complex and put it on a shelf so all can reach and walk away challenged wanting to *Dig In!* for themselves. I believe you will be strengthened and nourished and your heart will be recalibrated as you read along with Bert. Get ready to be impacted and go and influence your world for Christ!"

KEITH WALDROP
Pastor, The Table at Christ Community Church, Montgomery, Alabama

"What a breath of fresh air this devotional is! Bert Jones has masterfully offered the wealth of his theological insight as a launching pad to simply let the Scriptures speak. He manages to not only centralize the content of God's Word but teaches the reader how to study it along the way, in easily digestible sections. This is a much-needed tool in the hands of a follower of Jesus, young or old. *Dig In!* with Bert, and I assure you, you won't be disappointed!"

RYAN BASH
Lead Pastor, Brookside Church, Chillicothe, Ohio

"The Bible compares wisdom to gold, and this work is a shovel holding 35 years of gold. An outline structured as systematic theology and supplied with relevant Scripture awaits the reader willing to receive its treasure. As Christians believe the Bible is God's revelation to the world, this book leads us in discovery of its story and its counsel for life. Bert Jones guides the reader to the Scriptures from his 30 years of ministry wisdom, while the Holy Spirit guides the reader into the wisdom contained there."

W. BRIAN SHELTON, PHD
Dean of the School of Christian Studies, Asbury University

"*Dig In!* is a very fresh and creative devotional book that is filled with practical wisdom and deep insight gleaned from Bert's over 35 years of ministry. I highly recommend it to every Christ follower who seeks to grow deeper in their daily walk with Him."

REV. GARY MILLER
Retired Pastor and Evangelism and Church Revitalization Strategist, Alabama Baptist State Board of Missions

"Bert was creating Bible study outlines for us as teenagers at Asbury College, as youth leaders in our early ministries, at conferences, at mission meetings and at church services wherever he pastored in the United States and in Uruguay where I serve as a missionary pastor. I love Bert's heart for people around the world and continue to appreciate, value and enjoy the gift of his teaching ministry, friendship and marriage."

JOHN HAMILTON
Missionary with One Mission Society
Bert's college roommate

"For several years I had the opportunity to learn from watching Bert Jones lead and to experience firsthand his measured, wise and discerning leadership style. Often, I wondered how he became such an effective leader, but after reading—or rather experiencing—*Dig In!*, that question had been erased. It is no doubt due to the 35 years of his leadership being rooted so deeply in the Word, but not merely as facts to be memorized but principles to be applied and lived by. I am personally thankful to have this resource, but even more thankful that other kingdom leaders will have it to benefit from, too."

RODNEY ARNOLD
President, Missionary Church

"Bert's spiritual insights are both profound and practical, and his teaching is rooted firmly in God's Word. His ability to unpack Scripture in a way that is accessible and life-changing speaks to his dedication to understanding and living out the truths of the Bible."

MARTY GREENE
Business Owner

DEDICATION

My mother's birthday was January 2. My earliest memory of buying my mom a birthday present was purchasing her a daily devotional. She loved devotional books and faithfully spent time every day praying, reading her Bible and reading her devotional book for the year.

It wasn't intentional, but it became a tradition for me to buy her a different devotional book every year for her birthday. I was always searching for that perfect devotional she might enjoy and be uniquely different than one she had previously read. I looked for different authors, different perspectives and even different generations. Some were old classics and some were brand new.

One year she said to me, "Bert, you need to write your own devotional book. That is one I would love to have." At the moment, I passed it off, but I never forgot her request. It has always been in the back of my mind. I didn't write that devotional before she went to be with the Lord, but I never forgot her request.

I would like to honor my mother in this devotional by dedicating it to her, Lois VanGilder Jones. She was a wonderful wife, mother, pastor's wife and friend who lived out her commitment to Christ faithfully and consistently and had a meaningful quiet time with the Lord each day.

She instilled in me a love for Jesus and for God's Word, and this book is dedicated to her to honor and fulfill the request she made that day many years ago. May God use it to encourage you to *Dig In!* to His Word. Happy heavenly birthday, Mom. Thank you for inspiring me to daily *Dig In!* to God's Word and be a devoted follower of Christ.

The Christian Medical & Dental Associations was founded in 1931 and currently serves more than 13,000 members; coordinates a network of Christian healthcare professionals for personal and professional growth; sponsors student ministries in medical and dental schools; conducts overseas healthcare projects for underserved populations; addresses policies on healthcare, medical ethics and bioethical and human rights issues; distributes educational and inspirational resources; provides missionary healthcare professionals with continuing education resources; and conducts international academic exchange programs.

For more information:
Christian Medical & Dental Associations
P.O. Box 7500
Bristol, TN 37621-7500
888-230-2637
cmda.org • main@cmda.org

Editing by Mandi Morrin.
Cover design and interior layout by Ahaa! Design.

©2025 by Bert L. Jones and Christian Medical & Dental Associations
All rights reserved. No part of this publication may be reproduced in any form without written permission from Christian Medical & Dental Associations.

Scripture references marked (ESV) are taken from The ESV® Bible (The Holy Bible, English Standard Version®). ESV® Text Edition: 2016. Copyright © 2001 by Crossway, a publishing ministry of Good News Publishers. All rights reserved. Scripture references marked (NKJV) are taken from the New King James Version®. Copyright © 1982 by Thomas Nelson. Used by permission.

ISBN 978-1-7344968-6-4

Library of Congress Control Number 2024952041

Printed in the United States of America

TABLE OF CONTENTS

FOREWORD 11
INTRODUCTION 13
JANUARY 17
FEBRUARY 41
MARCH 65
APRIL 89
MAY 109
JUNE 131
JULY 155
AUGUST 179
SEPTEMBER 199
OCTOBER 223
NOVEMBER 249
DECEMBER 271
ACKNOWLEDGMENTS 295
TOPICAL INDEX 297

FOREWORD

Before His final departure, Jesus' last instructions to Peter centered on his call to be the first Christian pastor in history. "Do you love me? (three times)…Feed my sheep (three times)…Follow me (two times)" (John 21:15-22). The job description was profoundly simple—and simply profound. A pastor has three basic responsibilities:

1. Be passionately devoted to Jesus. (Do you love me?)
2. Nurture and feed God's flock. (Feed my sheep.)
3. Imitate Jesus' example. (Follow me.)

I marvel at the brevity. I gasp at the wisdom. I tremble at the responsibility. And I scratch my head in bewilderment at how many pastors today fall woefully short of these most basic requirements.

This explains why I am so thankful for Pastor Bert Jones and so happy to promote the book you hold in your hands! Bert belongs to a rare breed of pastors who have modeled their lives and ministries after the job description Jesus gave to Peter. Wherever he serves, Bert understands that *being* a pastor is more important than *doing* pastoral work. Although sheep are typically unaware as to what is involved in their care, they know when they are loved by their pastor—and when they are not. Bert always loves the sheep and labors tirelessly to feed them well! While numerous pastors today give out the predigested sermons they find on the internet or offer spiritual junk food that tastes great but has little nutritional value, Bert has a legacy for nurturing the flock of God with a steady diet of nutritional substance.

Bert's track record in ministry bears witness to how he faithfully obeys Jesus' demand to "Follow me." From the beginning, he has understood his calling in terms of modeling his life after Jesus, of imitating His example, particularly in the way Jesus renounced status, denied self and laid down His life for others. Bert understands pastoral ministry as did the apostle Paul: "So death is at work in us, but life in you" (2 Corinthians 4:12, ESV).

This devotional book is unlike any you have seen before. While most devotional writers prepare the meal and serve it to the reader ready-to-eat, Bert employs a different method. He gives *you* both the ingredients for the meal and the recipe to follow in cooking it. Then, he invites *you* to prepare the meal for yourself! For some, this will feel strange, and they may be tempted to slam the book shut and say, "I don't know how to cook; I can't do this!" Please, reconsider. Let Pastor Bert coax you through the process step by step. I assure you the effort will be well worthwhile!

Those who love to cook and feed themselves will discover this book is full of recipes they have never tried before. They will delight in the wide variety of gastronomical delicacies Bert is encouraging you to explore. And for pastors—oh my! The recipes Bert shares in this volume will give you enough preaching material to help you feed your sheep for years to come.

The prophet Amos spoke of a day when there would be a great global famine: "…not a famine of bread, nor a thirst for water, but of hearing the words of the Lord" (Amos 8:11, ESV). We are living in those days now! Ironically, never have we had more Bibles, more Christian books or more access to spiritual resources than today. And yet, never has there more spiritual malnourishment. Yes, even in Bible-believing churches, countless people struggle with spiritual eating disorders of every imaginable kind. The sheep are famished.

One of the marks of physical maturity is when a person assumes the responsibility of feeding himself. So it is in the spiritual life (see Hebrews 5:11-14). Pastor Bert is inviting you to discover the joy of taking God's Word and feeding yourself. So, what's stopping you? Turn the page and *Dig In*!

STAN KEY
OneWay Ministries – Minister at Large

INTRODUCTION

The devotional you hold in your hand is designed to be a tool to fuel your hunger and thirst for God's Word. As you *Dig In!* to this devotional, realize it is intended to serve more as a "shovel" than a "spoon."

So often, devotionals are created to spoon feed your daily spiritual nourishment to you. They offer a fast grasp of the topic, but they often lack depth and breadth on matters of discipleship and the deeper Christian life.

When I began praying about this project, my desire was to develop a devotional that the individual reading the study could determine the depth of their time in the Word. I wanted the reader to carry the responsibility of the heavy lifting.

I have been working on the concept of this devotional book for several years, and I believe it is different than what typically appears in daily devotionals I purchased for my mom over the years.

I have been in full-time ministry since 1989. During those years of ministry, I have given thousands of messages, outlines, devotionals and sermons in settings all over the world. I have acquired dozens of notebooks with sermon outline ideas I haven't yet taken to the pulpit. Those ideas are simmering on the back burner for future messages.

An evangelist who influenced me when I first started into the ministry gave me two pieces of advice. Log every sermon you preach and keep track of where you preached it, and save every message idea the Lord gives you and file every sermon or talk you give. I've done that since I started my ministry years ago, and these daily devotionals are the fruit of that advice.

For this devotional, I went back through those stacks of notebooks and electronic copies of messages I have had the opportunity to preach across the country and around the world. And then I am giving you the starting point to have some quality time alone with the Lord in His Word.

You hold in your hand the shovel to *Dig In!* Each day is an outline and Scriptures you can use to explore God's Word. I have included several references for you to search the Scriptures, but what I have given you doesn't even begin to scratch the surface of how God desires to speak to you and what God desires to show you as you study His Word.

My goal in this book is to provide content to spark the Holy Spirit to speak directly to you, not commentary to spring the thoughts of someone else who did the digging for you. As they say, Scripture is the best way to interpret Scripture. The more you investigate God's Word, the more information and insight you will gain to walk in a way honoring and pleasing to God.

I challenge you use this devotional daily. As you begin your devotions, pray and ask God to speak to you (1 Samuel 3:9). I challenge you to consider the topic, reflect on the principles and points of the outlines and then gain new insights as you work your way through the passages of Scripture provided each day. Take time to explore your own cross-referencing on these spiritual topics.

I pray this daily discipleship devotional will influence and impact in your personal walk with Christ. May 1 Peter 2:2-3 be the reality of your spiritual journey.

"Like newborn infants, long for the pure spiritual milk, that by it you may grow up into salvation—if indeed you have tasted that the Lord is good."

—1 Peter 2:2-3, ESV

AUTHOR'S NOTE
and Code for Bible Translations

As you work through this devotional, you will notice an abbreviation for a specific Bible translation is included with each day. This will be your translation guide for the day to help you know which translation will be the primary source for Scriptures, unless otherwise noted. In some cases, even though a primary translation for the day is noted, a different translation will be listed beside a specific passage of Scripture.

Here is the list of abbreviations:

- **AMP:** Amplified Bible
- **ESV:** English Standard Version
- **HCSB:** Holman Christian Standard Bible
- **KJV:** King James Version
- **MSG:** The Message
- **NASB:** New American Standard Bible
- **(NIV):** New International Version
- **(NKJV):** New King James Version
- **(NLT):** New Living Translation
- **TLB:** Living Bible

You will also notice each day also includes a place for notes and observations. I encourage you to use your Bible study tools as you *Dig In* and make notes on other passages of Scripture that speak to the subject matter at hand. The Scriptures listed each day only begin to scratch the surface. Take the time to search for more.

> *"Oh, the depth of the riches both of the wisdom and knowledge of God! How unsearchable are His judgments and His ways past finding out!"*
>
> —Romans 11:33, (NKJV)

Questions to Ask as You Dig In to These Scriptures

1. How did God speak to you through this passage? What caught your attention?

2. What observations did you discover as you read through the passage (who, what, when, where, why and how)?

3. What is the meaning or interpretation of this passage of Scripture?

4. Does your study Bible give any key insights into the passage that you want to share?

5. What are the takeaway lessons you learned from the passage?

6. Are there any parallel passages or cross-reference Scriptures that give clarity or confirmation to the passage?

7. What would it look like if you put this passage into practice and applied it this week?

JANUARY 1

Five Sin Problems That Cause Us Trouble James 5:13-20 (NIV)

1. ORIGINAL SIN
- ☐ Genesis 3
- ☐ Romans 3:23
- ☐ Psalm 51:5
- ☐ Genesis 8:21
- ☐ Romans 5:12

2. GENERATIONAL SIN
- ☐ Exodus 20:5
- ☐ Exodus 34:6-7
- ☐ Numbers 14:18
- ☐ Jeremiah 32:18
- ☐ Nehemiah 1:6-9

3. INTENTIONAL SIN (willful)
- ☐ James 4:17
- ☐ Hebrews 10:26
- ☐ Numbers 15:30-31
- ☐ 1 Samuel 15:23 (NKJV)
- ☐ Psalm 19:13

4. CONFIDENTIAL SIN (secret, private, hidden or kept concealed)
- ☐ Psalm 90:8
- ☐ Proverbs 28:13
- ☐ Numbers 32:23
- ☐ Luke 12:1-2
- ☐ Jeremiah 16:17-18
- ☐ Hebrews 4:13
- ☐ Romans 2:16

5. UNINTENTIONAL SIN
- ☐ 1 Timothy 1:13
- ☐ Acts 3:17-19
- ☐ Leviticus 4:2-3
- ☐ Leviticus 4:13-14
- ☐ Leviticus 5:17-18
- ☐ Numbers 15:27-29

JANUARY 2
Where We Can Find Encouragement
2 Thessalonians 2:16 (NIV)

1. **FROM THE SCRIPTURES**
   - ☐ Romans 15:4-5

2. **FROM THE PREACHING OF GOD'S WORD**
   - ☐ Acts 13:15 (NLT)
   - ☐ Acts 20:2

3. **FROM THE PROPHECY OF SCRIPTURE**
   - ☐ 1 Corinthians 14:3,31

4. **FROM OTHER BELIEVERS**
   - ☐ Acts 4:36
   - ☐ 2 Corinthians 7:5-13 (NLT)
   - ☐ Philemon 7

5. **FROM THE FAITH OF GOD'S PEOPLE**
   - ☐ Romans 1:12

6. **FROM BELONGING TO CHRIST**
   - ☐ Philippians 2:1

7. **FROM GOD'S LOVE AND DISCIPLINE**
   - ☐ Hebrews 12:5

JANUARY 3
Symbols of the Spirit: [Part 1] (NLT)

1. **DOVE**
   - ☐ Mark 1:10
   - ☐ Matthew 3:16-17
   - ☐ Luke 3:22
   - ☐ John 1:32

2. WIND OR BREATH
- [ ] John 3:8
- [ ] Acts 2:2
- [ ] Acts 4:31
- [ ] John 20:20-22
- [ ] Ezekiel 37:9-14

3. FIRE
- [ ] Matthew 3:11
- [ ] Luke 3:16-17
- [ ] 1 Thessalonians 5:19 (NKJV)

JANUARY 4
Symbols of the Spirit: [Part 2] (NLT)

1. TONGUES AND PROPHECY
- [ ] Acts 2:3
- [ ] Acts 19:6
- [ ] 1 Corinthians 12:10
- [ ] 1 Corinthians 14:1

2. WATER
- [ ] John 3:5
- [ ] John 7:37-39
- [ ] John 4:14
- [ ] Ezekiel 36:25-27

3. OIL
- [ ] 1 Samuel 16:13
- [ ] Isaiah 61:1
- [ ] Luke 4:18
- [ ] Acts 10:38
- [ ] 1 John 2:20 (NKJV)

4. FRUIT
- [ ] Romans 8:23
- [ ] Galatians 5:22-23

5. SEAL OR GUARANTEE
- [ ] Ephesians 1:13-14 (NKJV)
- [ ] Ephesians 4:30
- [ ] 2 Corinthians 1:22

NOTES

JANUARY 5
Three Kinds of Peace
Romans 15:33 (NKJV)

1. **PEACE WITH GOD**
   - ☐ Romans 5:1
   - ☐ Ephesians 2:11-17

2. **PEACE OF GOD**
   - ☐ Philippians 4:7-9
   - ☐ Colossians 3:15
   - ☐ John 14:27

3. **PEACE FROM GOD**
   - ☐ 2 Corinthians 2:13 (NLT)
   - ☐ Romans 1:7
   - ☐ 1 Corinthians 1:3
   - ☐ 2 Thessalonians 3:16
   - ☐ Isaiah 26:3

JANUARY 6
Three People Who Ask One Question
Galatians 2:15-21 (NKJV)

"What must I do to be saved?"

1. **THE LAWYER WHO WANTED TO JUSTIFY HIMSELF**
   - ☐ Luke 10:25-30

2. **THE RULER WHO WANTED TO JUST MAKE IT BY**
   - ☐ Luke 18:18-27

3. **THE JAILER WHO WANTED TO BE JUSTIFIED**
   - ☐ Acts 16:25-31

NOTES

JANUARY 7
The Three Prayers for Revival
John 11:1-11 (NKJV)

1. **REVIVE THY WORK**
   - ☐ Habakkuk 3:2
   - ☐ Psalm 44
   - ☐ Deuteronomy 3:24
   - ☐ Psalm 90:13-17

2. **REVIVE US AGAIN**
   - ☐ Psalm 85:6
   - ☐ Psalm 80:18
   - ☐ Hosea 6:1-3

3. **REVIVE ME**
   - ☐ Psalm 138:7
   - ☐ Psalm 71:20
   - ☐ Psalm 119:25,37,40,88,107,149
   - ☐ Psalm 51:10
   - ☐ Isaiah 57:15

JANUARY 8
The Three Levels of Evil
Romans 12:17-21 (NKJV)

1. **THE LEVEL WHERE YOU RETURN EVIL FOR GOOD**
   - ☐ Psalm 35:12
   - ☐ Psalm 38:19-20
   - ☐ Psalm 109:4-5
   - ☐ Proverbs 17:13

2. **THE LEVEL WHERE YOU RETURN EVIL FOR EVIL**
   - ☐ Matthew 5:38-39
   - ☐ Romans 12:17-19
   - ☐ 1 Thessalonians 5:15

3. THE LEVEL WHERE YOU RETURN GOOD FOR EVIL
- ☐ Romans 12:21
- ☐ Matthew 5:43-48
- ☐ Genesis 50:20-21
- ☐ 1 Peter 3:9

JANUARY 9

The Second Coming: [Part 1] (NKJV)

In preparation for the Lord's return:

1. WE SHOULD BE PATIENT
- ☐ James 5:8
- ☐ 2 Peter 3:8-10 (NLT)

2. WE SHOULD BE READY
- ☐ Matthew 24:44
- ☐ Luke 12:38 (NLT)

3. WE SHOULD BE WATCHING
- ☐ Matthew 25:13
- ☐ Luke 12:37
- ☐ 1 Thessalonians 5:6
- ☐ 1 Peter 4:7
- ☐ Titus 2:12-13

4. WE SHOULD BE BUSY
- ☐ Luke 12:43
- ☐ Luke 19:13

5. WE SHOULD BE LONGING AND WAITING
- ☐ 2 Timothy 4:7-8
- ☐ 1 Corinthians 1:7
- ☐ Philippians 3:20
- ☐ 1 Thessalonians 1:8-10
- ☐ Hebrews 9:28
- ☐ Jude 1:21

6. WE SHOULD AVOID JUDGING OTHERS
- ☐ 1 Corinthians 4:5

NOTES

JANUARY 10

The Second Coming: [Part 2] (NKJV)

In preparation for the Lord's return:

1. **WE SHOULD BE OBEDIENT TO GOD'S COMMANDMENTS**
   - ☐ 1 Timothy 6:12-14

2. **WE SHOULD BE ABIDING IN HIM**
   - ☐ 1 John 2:28

3. **WE SHOULD BE BLAMELESS**
   - ☐ 1 Timothy 6:13-14
   - ☐ Philippians 1:10
   - ☐ 1 Thessalonians 3:13
   - ☐ 1 Thessalonians 5:23
   - ☐ Titus 2:11-13

4. **WE SHOULD CONTINUE TO HOPE**
   - ☐ 1 Peter 1:3-5
   - ☐ 1 Peter 1:13
   - ☐ 1 John 3:2-3

5. **WE SHOULD PROCLAIM THE LORD'S DEATH UNTIL HE COMES**
   - ☐ 1 Corinthians 11:26
   - ☐ 2 Timothy 4:1-2
   - ☐ 2 Peter 1:16

6. **WE SHOULD ENCOURAGE ONE ANOTHER AND NOT BE UNSETTLED**
   - ☐ 1 Thessalonians 4:15-5:11
   - ☐ 2 Thessalonians 2:1-2

JANUARY 11

The Purpose Statements of Jesus: [Part 1] (NKJV)

1. **HE CAME TO FULFILL PROPHECY**
   - ☐ Matthew 5:17-18
   - ☐ Romans 8:3-4

2. **HE CAME TO SEEK AND SAVE THE LOST**
   - ☐ Luke 19:10
   - ☐ 1 Timothy 1:15
   - ☐ Luke 9:56
   - ☐ John 3:17
   - ☐ 1 John 4:14

3. **HE CAME TO GIVE HIS LIFE AS A RANSOM FOR MANY**
   - ☐ Matthew 20:28
   - ☐ John 12:27

4. **HE CAME TO CALL SINNERS TO REPENTANCE**
   - ☐ Mark 2:17
   - ☐ Luke 5:32

5. **HE CAME TO SERVE**
   - ☐ Mark 10:45
   - ☐ Matthew 20:28
   - ☐ Philippians 2:5-11

6. **HE CAME TO PREACH THE GOOD NEWS**
   - ☐ Luke 4:18-19
   - ☐ Luke 4:43
   - ☐ Mark 1:38
   - ☐ January 12

NOTES

JANUARY 12

The Purpose Statements of Jesus: [Part 2] (NKJV)

1. **HE CAME TO BRING DIVISION**
   - ☐ Luke 12:51
   - ☐ Matthew 10:34-36

2. **HE CAME TO REVEAL THE FATHER TO HUMANKIND**
   - ☐ John 1:18
   - ☐ John 12:45
   - ☐ John 14:9
   - ☐ Matthew 11:27

3. **HE CAME TO DO THE FATHER'S WILL**
   - ☐ John 6:38
   - ☐ John 17:4
   - ☐ Hebrews 10:9

4. **HE CAME TO JUDGE**
   - ☐ John 9:39
   - ☐ Luke 12:49

5. **HE CAME THAT WE MIGHT HAVE ABUNDANT LIFE**
   - ☐ John 10:10

6. **HE CAME AS THE LIGHT OF THE WORLD**
   - ☐ John 8:12
   - ☐ John 9:5
   - ☐ John 12:46

JANUARY 13

The Purpose Statements of Jesus: [Part 3] (NKJV)

1. **HE CAME TO BEAR WITNESS TO THE TRUTH**
   - ☐ John 18:37
   - ☐ John 14:6

2. **HE CAME TO GIVE US AN EXAMPLE**
   - ☐ 1 Peter 2:21
   - ☐ Matthew 11:29

3. **HE CAME TO TAKE AWAY OUR SIN**
   - ☐ 1 John 3:5
   - ☐ John 1:29
   - ☐ 1 Peter 2:24
   - ☐ Hebrews 9:26

4. **HE CAME TO DESTROY THE WORKS OF THE DEVIL**
   - ☐ 1 John 3:8
   - ☐ Hebrews 2:14
   - ☐ Romans 16:20
   - ☐ Colossians 2:15

JANUARY 14

Suggestions for Serving the Lord (NKJV)

1. **SERVE THE LORD WITH GLADNESS**
   - ☐ Psalm 100:2
   - ☐ Deuteronomy 28:47

2. **SERVE THE LORD WITH ALL HUMILITY**
   - ☐ Acts 20:19

3. **SERVE THE LORD FAITHFULLY**
   - ☐ 1 Samuel 12:24

4. **SERVE THE LORD WITH FERVENCY**
   - ☐ Romans 12:11

5. **SERVE THE LORD WITH WHOLEHEARTED DEVOTION**
   - ☐ 1 Chronicles 28:9
   - ☐ Deuteronomy 10:12
   - ☐ Joshua 22:5

6. **SERVE THE LORD WITHOUT DISTRACTION**
   - ☐ 1 Corinthians 7:35

JANUARY 15

Living to Please God: [Part 1] *Romans 12:2 (NLT)*

God is pleased when:

1. **WE TURN FROM SIN AND TURN TO HIM**
   - ☐ Ezekiel 18:23
   - ☐ Ezekiel 33:11
   - ☐ Psalm 5:4

2. **WE USE THE MEASURE OF FAITH HE GIVES US**
   - ☐ Hebrews 11:6
   - ☐ Hebrews 10:38

3. **WE ARE OBEDIENT TO HIS WORD**
   - ☐ 1 John 3:22
   - ☐ Deuteronomy 12:28

4. **WE WALK WITH HIM DAILY IN DEVOTION**
   - ☐ Genesis 5:24
   - ☐ Hebrews 11:5
   - ☐ Colossians 1:9-10

5. **WE ARE SPIRITUALLY MINDED NOT EARTHLY FOCUSED**
   - ☐ Romans 8:5-8

JANUARY 16

Living to Please God: [Part 2]

1 Thessalonians 4:1-3 (NLT)

God is pleased when:

1. **WE HAVE A HEALTHY FEAR OF THE LORD**
   - ☐ Psalm 147:10-11

2. **WE IMITATE HIS SON JESUS**
   - ☐ Matthew 3:17 (NKJV)
   - ☐ John 8:29

3. **WE STRIVE TO ACCOMPLISH HIS WILL**
   - ☐ Hebrews 13:21

4. **WE DO GOOD FOR OTHERS**
   - ☐ Hebrews 13:15-16
   - ☐ 1 Timothy 5:3-4

5. **WE MEDITATE AND COMMUNICATE HIS THOUGHTS**
   - ☐ Psalm 19:14
   - ☐ Psalm 104:34

JANUARY 17

Living to Please God: [Part 3]

Ephesians 5:10 (NLT)

God is pleased when:

1. **WE GIVE HIM PRAISE AND THANKSGIVING**
   - ☐ Psalm 69:30-31

2. **WE CARE MORE ABOUT PLEASING HIM THAN OTHERS**
   - ☐ 1 Thessalonians 2:4
   - ☐ Galatians 1:10

3. **WHEN WE PRAY**
   ☐ 1 Timothy 2:1-3

4. **WE LIVE IN THE POWER OF THE HOLY SPIRIT**
   ☐ Romans 14:17-18

5. **WE HUMBLE OURSELVES**
   ☐ Psalm 149:4 (NKJV)
   ☐ Psalm 51:16-17 (NIV)
   ☐ 2 Corinthians 5:9-10
   ☐ Philippians 2:13

JANUARY 18
Commands for Spirit-filled Living
Ephesians 5:18 (NIV)

1. **WALK IN THE SPIRIT**
   ☐ Galatians 5:16

2. **BE LED BY THE SPIRIT**
   ☐ Galatians 5:18
   ☐ Romans 8:12-14

3. **LIVE BY THE SPIRIT**
   ☐ Galatians 5:25

4. **KEEP IN STEP WITH THE SPIRIT**
   ☐ Galatians 5:25

5. **SOW TO PLEASE THE SPIRIT**
   ☐ Galatians 6:8

JANUARY 19
Three Common Ways We Commit Sin (NLT)

We have to understand we all commit sin:

1. **INITIALLY** (all are born into sin)
   - ☐ Romans 5:12
   - ☐ Romans 3:23

2. **IGNORANTLY**
   - ☐ Hebrews 9:7

3. **INTENTIONALLY** (willfully)
   - ☐ Hebrews 10:26
   - ☐ James 4:17
   - ☐ 1 John 1:9

JANUARY 20
Five Ways to Overcome the Devil (NKJV)

1. **STAND**
   - ☐ Ephesians 6:13-14

2. **WRESTLE**
   - ☐ Ephesians 6:12

3. **RESIST**
   - ☐ James 4:7

4. **GIVE NO PLACE**
   - ☐ Ephesians 4:26-27

5. **PRAY**
   - ☐ Ephesians 6:18

NOTES

JANUARY 21

Five Things You Need to Know About God's Gift of Salvation (NKJV)

1. **IT IS GIVEN OUT OF UNCONDITIONAL LOVE**
   - ☐ John 3:16

2. **IT IS A FREE GIFT**
   - ☐ Romans 5:15
   - ☐ Romans 8:32
   - ☐ Acts 8:20

3. **IT IS A GIFT BASED ON GRACE, NOT WORKS**
   - ☐ Ephesians 2:8

4. **IT IS AN INDESCRIBABLE GIFT**
   - ☐ 2 Corinthians 9:15
   - ☐ John 4:10

5. **IT IS AN ETERNAL GIFT**
   - ☐ Romans 6:23
   - ☐ John 3:36
   - ☐ 1 John 5:11-12

JANUARY 22

Seven Things God Does With Sin
Matthew 1:21 (NKJV)

1. **HE CONVICTS US OF OUR SINS**
   - ☐ Jude 15
   - ☐ John 16:8

2. **HE FORGIVES US OF OUR SINS**
   - ☐ Matthew 9:2-6
   - ☐ Ephesians 1:7-8
   - ☐ Colossians 1:13-14
   - ☐ Psalm 32:1
   - ☐ Romans 4:7

3. **HE CLEANSES US FROM OUR SINS**
   - ☐ 1 John 1:9
   - ☐ Acts 3:19
   - ☐ Psalm 51:9

4. **HE REMOVES OUR SINS**
   - ☐ Psalm 103:12
   - ☐ 2 Corinthians 5:17

5. **HE REMEMBERS OUR SINS NO MORE**
   - ☐ Hebrews 8:12
   - ☐ Hebrews 10:17
   - ☐ Ezekiel 33:16
   - ☐ Micah 7:19
   - ☐ Isaiah 43:25
   - ☐ Jeremiah 31:34

6. **HE MAKES THEM WHITE AS SNOW**
   - ☐ Isaiah 1:18

7. **HE GIVES US VICTORY OVER OUR SINS**
   - ☐ 1 Corinthians 15:55-57

JANUARY 23
Seven Things You Cannot Live Without (NKJV)

1. **THE SHEDDING OF BLOOD**
   - ☐ Hebrews 9:22

2. **FAITH**
   - ☐ Hebrews 11:6

3. **WORKS**
   - ☐ James 2:26

4. **HOLINESS**
   - ☐ Hebrews 12:14

5. **LOVE**
   - ☐ 1 Corinthians 13:1-2

6. **DISCIPLINE**
   - [ ] Hebrews 12:8

7. **JESUS**
   - [ ] John 15:5
   - [ ] Ephesians 2:12-13

JANUARY 24
Eight Things We Should Do With Sin
Psalm 32:1-11 (NKJV)

1. **REALIZE AND ADMIT WE ARE ALL SINNERS**
   - [ ] Romans 3:23
   - [ ] 1 John 1:8-10
   - [ ] Psalm 32:5

2. **MOURN AND BE SORROWFUL FOR OUR SIN**
   - [ ] Matthew 5:4
   - [ ] 2 Corinthians 7:10
   - [ ] James 4:9

3. **REPENT AND BE FORGIVEN OF OUR SIN**
   - [ ] 1 John 1:9
   - [ ] Acts 3:19
   - [ ] Luke 13:2-3
   - [ ] 2 Peter 3:9

4. **TURN FROM OUR SINFUL WAYS**
   - [ ] Romans 6:1-14
   - [ ] John 8:1-11
   - [ ] 1 John 2:1

5. **REMOVE ANY HINDRANCES CAUSING US TO SIN**
   - [ ] Matthew 5:29-30
   - [ ] Hebrews 12:1

6. **REPLACE ANY SIN WITH HIM**
   - [ ] Romans 6:6-14
   - [ ] Galatians 2:20
   - [ ] Galatians 5:22-23
   - [ ] Psalm 119:11

7. **STAY AWAY FROM SIN AND DON'T GO NEAR IT**
   - ☐ Ephesians 4:26-27
   - ☐ Ephesians 5:11

8. **DO NOT PRACTICE OR APPROVE OF IT**
   - ☐ Romans 1:32
   - ☐ 1 John 3:3-10

JANUARY 25
Six Warnings Regarding the Holy Spirit *Psalm 51:11 (NKJV)*

1. **DO NOT ABUSE THE TEMPLE OF THE HOLY SPIRIT**
   - ☐ 1 Corinthians 3:16
   - ☐ 1 Corinthians 6:18-20

2. **DO NOT RESIST THE HOLY SPIRIT**
   - ☒ Acts 7:51
   - ☐ 1 Thessalonians 4:8

3. **DO NOT GRIEVE THE HOLY SPIRIT**
   - ☐ Ephesians 4:30
   - ☐ Isaiah 63:10
   - ☐ Genesis 6:1-6

4. **DO NOT QUENCH THE HOLY SPIRIT**
   - ☐ 1 Thessalonians 5:19

5. **DO NOT BLASPHEME AGAINST THE HOLY SPIRIT**
   - ☐ Hebrews 10:26-29
   - ☐ Matthew 12:31-32

6. **DO NOT LIE TO THE HOLY SPIRIT**
   - ☐ Acts 5:3

NOTES

Acts 7:51 "You stiff-necked people, uncircumcised in heart and ears, you always resist the holy spirit. As your fathers did, so do you.

JANUARY 26
Five Keys to Being Justified [NKJV]

We are justified by:

1. **BELIEVING IN GOD**
   - ☐ Acts 16:33-34
   - ☐ Acts 13:39
   - ☐ Romans 10:10

2. **HIS BLOOD**
   - ☐ Romans 5:8-9

3. **FAITH**
   - ☐ Romans 3:27-28

   FOUR TIMES THE WORD SAYS THE JUST SHALL LIVE BY FAITH:
   - ☐ Habakkuk 2:4
   - ☐ Romans 1:17
   - ☐ Galatians 3:11
   - ☐ Hebrews 10:38

4. **GRACE**
   - ☐ Romans 3:24
   - ☐ Titus 3:7

5. **HIS SPIRIT**
   - ☐ 1 Corinthians 6:11

JANUARY 27
God's Desire [NLT]

1. **TO BE FOR US**
   - ☐ Romans 8:31
   - ☐ Nehemiah 4:20
   - ☐ Ephesians 2:4 (NIV)
   - ☐ Ephesians 5:1-2 (NIV)

2. **TO BE WITH US**
   - [ ] Matthew 1:23 (NKJV)
   - [ ] 2 Chronicles 13:12
   - [ ] 2 Chronicles 20:17
   - [ ] Joshua 1:9
   - [ ] Psalm 46:7-11
   - [ ] Isaiah 7:14
   - [ ] Isaiah 8:10
   - [ ] Isaiah 41:10
   - [ ] 2 Timothy 4:17

3. **TO BE IN US**
   - [ ] John 14:15-21
   - [ ] John 15:4-7
   - [ ] 1 Corinthians 3:16
   - [ ] 1 Corinthians 6:19
   - [ ] 2 Corinthians 6:7
   - [ ] Colossians 1:27
   - [ ] Romans 8:9-11

4. **TO WORK THROUGH US**
   - [ ] 2 Corinthians 2:14 (NKJV)
   - [ ] 2 Corinthians 5:20

JANUARY 28
Whoever (NKJV)

1. **BELIEVES**
   - [ ] John 3:16

2. **CALLS**
   - [ ] Acts 2:21

3. **COMES**
   - [ ] Revelation 22:17

JANUARY 29

The "I Am" Statements of Jesus in John
John 8:58 (NKJV)

1. **I AM THE BREAD OF LIFE**
   - ☐ John 6:35-48

2. **I AM THE LIGHT OF THE WORLD**
   - ☐ John 8:12
   - ☐ John 9:5

3. **I AM THE DOOR**
   - ☐ John 10:9

4. **I AM THE GOOD SHEPHERD**
   - ☐ John 10:11

5. **I AM THE RESURRECTION AND THE LIFE**
   - ☐ John 11:25

6. **I AM THE WAY, THE TRUTH AND THE LIFE**
   - ☐ John 14:6

7. **I AM THE TRUE VINE**
   - ☐ John 15:1

JANUARY 30

Five Responsibilities We Have Toward Those in Authority
Romans 13:1-7 (NKJV)

1. **NOT TO SPEAK UNKINDLY AGAINST THOSE IN AUTHORITY**
   - ☐ Acts 23:1-5
   - ☐ Exodus 22:28

2. **NOT TO ACCUSE SOMEONE IN AUTHORITY WITHOUT THE PROPER PROOF**
   - ☐ 1 Timothy 5:19

3. **PRAY FOR THOSE IN AUTHORITY**
   - ☐ 1 Timothy 2:1-2

4. **RESPECT THOSE IN AUTHORITY**
   - ☐ Romans 13:7

5. **SUBMIT TO THOSE IN AUTHORITY**
   - ☐ Romans 13:1-2
   - ☐ Hebrews 13:17

   a. Children are to submit in obedience to their parents
   - ☐ Ephesians 6:1

   b. Wives are to submit to their husbands
   - ☐ Ephesians 5:22-24

   c. The church is to be submissive to the appointed leaders and to Christ
   - ☐ Hebrews 13:17
   - ☐ Ephesians 5:24

   d. Servants are to submit to their masters
   - ☐ Ephesians 6:5-8
   - ☐ 1 Peter 2:17-18

   e. Individuals are to submit to the government
   - ☐ Romans 13:1-7
   - ☐ Titus 3:1

   f. Believers are to submit to God
   - ☐ Hebrews 12:9
   - ☐ James 4:7

NOTES

JANUARY 31

The Holy Spirit is Given to Those Who *Acts 8:9-21 (NKJV)*

1. **REPENT**
   - ☐ Acts 8:22-23
   - ☐ Matthew 3:11
   - ☐ Acts 2:38

2. **ASK**
   - ☐ Luke 11:9-13
   - ☐ Ephesians 1:17 (NIV)
   - ☐ Colossians 1:9 (NIV)

3. **WAIT**
   - ☐ Acts 1:4-5
   - ☐ Acts 1:8
   - ☐ Acts 2:1-4
   - ☐ Luke 24:49

4. **OBEY**
   - ☐ John 14:15-21
   - ☐ Acts 5:32
   - ☐ 1 John 3:24

5. **HAVE FAITH**
   - ☐ Galatians 3:2-14
   - ☐ Acts 6:5
   - ☐ Acts 11:24

6. **THIRST**
   - ☐ John 7:37-39

7. **RECEIVE**
   - ☐ John 20:22
   - ☐ Acts 19:2-6
   - ☐ John 14:17

FEBRUARY

FEBRUARY 1
Trust Him Even When *Psalm 62:8 (NLT)*

1. **YOU CAN'T SEE HIM**
   - ☐ 1 Peter 1:8

2. **YOU DON'T UNDERSTAND**
   - ☐ Proverbs 3:5-6
   - ☐ Psalm 28:7,26

3. **YOU ARE UNSURE HOW THINGS WILL WORK OUT**
   - ☐ Psalm 37:3-9

4. **YOU ARE AFRAID**
   - ☐ Psalm 56:3-11
   - ☐ Isaiah 12:2

5. **YOU ARE UNSETTLED**
   - ☐ Isaiah 26:3-4

6. **YOU ARE TIRED AND WEARY**
   - ☐ Isaiah 40:31

7. **YOU FEEL HELPLESS AND THINGS LOOK HOPELESS**
   - ☐ Jeremiah 17:7
   - ☐ Romans 15:13

FEBRUARY 2
The Three Types of Godliness (NKJV)

1. **UNGODLINESS**
   - ☐ Romans 1:18
   - ☐ Titus 2:12
   - ☐ 2 Timothy 2:16

NOTES

2. FORM OF GODLINESS
- [ ] 2 Timothy 3:5

3. TRUE GODLINESS
- [ ] Acts 3:12
- [ ] 1 Timothy 2:2
- [ ] 1 Timothy 4:7-8
- [ ] 1 Timothy 6:3-6,11
- [ ] 2 Peter 1:3,6-7
- [ ] 2 Peter 3:11

FEBRUARY 3
God Is Able To (NKJV)

1. DELIVER
- [ ] Daniel 3:16-17

2. FULFILL HIS PROMISES
- [ ] Romans 4:20-21

3. MAKE ALL GRACE ABOUND
- [ ] 2 Corinthians 9:8

4. DO EXCEEDINGLY ABUNDANTLY MORE
- [ ] Ephesians 3:20

5. SUBDUE ALL THINGS
- [ ] Philippians 3:20-21

6. GUARD
- [ ] 2 Timothy 1:12

7. KEEP FROM FALLING
- [ ] Jude 1:24
- [ ] 1 Corinthians 1:8

NOTES

FEBRUARY 4

Satan's Strategy *1 Peter 5:8-9 (NKJV)*

Satan comes:

1. **IMMEDIATELY**
   - ☐ Mark 4:15

2. **UNEXPECTANTLY**
   - ☐ Matthew 13:25-30

3. **REPEATEDLY**
   - ☐ Luke 4:13

BEFORE YOU PUT THE SHOVEL DOWN
   - ☐ Ephesians 6:10-18

FEBRUARY 5

Three Examples of Forgiveness (NKJV)

1. **JESUS**
   - ☐ Luke 23:34

2. **STEPHEN**
   - ☐ Acts 7:59-60

3. **PAUL**
   - ☐ 2 Timothy 4:16

BEFORE YOU PUT THE SHOVEL DOWN
   - ☐ Ephesians 4:31-32

FEBRUARY 6

Bless the Lord (NKJV)

1. **AT ALL TIMES**
   - ☐ Psalm 34:1
   - ☐ Psalm 145:2

2. **ALL YOU SERVANTS**
   - ☐ Psalm 134:1
   - ☐ Psalm 103:21

3. **WITH ALL THAT IS WITHIN ME**
   - ☐ Psalm 103:1

4. **FOR ALL HIS WORKS**
   - ☐ Psalm 103:2, 21-22
   - ☐ Psalm 145:10

NOTE the Five "Whos" *(Psalm 103:3-5)*

a. Who forgives all your iniquities

b. Who heals all your diseases

c. Who redeems your life from destruction

d. Who crowns you with lovingkindness and tender mercies

e. Who satisfies your mouth with good things

BEFORE YOU PUT THE SHOVEL DOWN
- ☐ Haggai 2:19

NOTES

FEBRUARY 7

Unless... (NKJV)

1. **YOU REPENT**
   - [ ] Luke 13:1-5

2. **YOU BE CONVERTED**
   - [ ] Matthew 18:2-3

3. **YOU BE BORN AGAIN**
   - [ ] John 3:3
   - [ ] 1 John 3:8-9
   - [ ] 1 John 5:1-13,18

4. **YOU BE BORN OF WATER AND THE SPIRIT**
   - [ ] John 3:5

5. **YOU EAT THE FLESH**
   - [ ] John 6:53

6. **YOUR RIGHTEOUSNESS EXCEEDS**
   - [ ] Matthew 5:20

7. **YOU ABIDE IN ME**
   - [ ] John 15:4-6

FEBRUARY 8

Four Areas God Will Judge You (NKJV)

1. **YOUR DEEDS**
   - [ ] 2 Corinthians 5:10

2. **YOUR WORDS**
   - [ ] Matthew 12:36-37

3. **YOUR MOTIVES**
   - [ ] 1 Corinthians 4:5

4. **YOUR TALENTS AND HOW YOU USED THEM**
   - [ ] Matthew 25:14-29

FEBRUARY 9
Three Levels of Righteousness (NKJV)

1. **UNRIGHTEOUSNESS**
   - ☐ Romans 1:18,29
   - ☐ 1 Corinthians 6:9
   - ☐ 2 Thessalonians 2:9-12
   - ☐ 2 Peter 2:13-15
   - ☐ 1 John 1:9
   - ☐ 1 John 5:17

2. **SELF-RIGHTEOUSNESS**
   - ☐ Matthew 5:20
   - ☐ Matthew 9:13
   - ☐ Matthew 25:37
   - ☐ Luke 18:9
   - ☐ Philippians 3:8-9

3. **HIS RIGHTEOUSNESS**
   - ☐ Romans 3:21-22
   - ☐ Romans 4:3-6
   - ☐ Romans 5:19
   - ☐ 2 Corinthians 5:21

FEBRUARY 10
Three Things I Must Do Today
Hebrews 3:7-15 (NKJV)

1. **I MUST HEAR HIS VOICE**
   - ☐ Hebrews 3:7,15
   - ☐ Mark 4:24
   - ☐ John 10:27

2. **I MUST EXHORT AND ENCOURAGE OTHERS**
   - ☐ Hebrews 3:13
   - ☐ Hebrews 10:25
   - ☐ Acts 14:21-22

3. I MUST KEEP A TENDER HEART
- ☐ Hebrews 3:13-15
- ☐ 2 Chronicles 34:26-27
- ☐ Ephesians 4:32
- ☐ Colossians 3:12
- ☐ 1 Peter 3:8

FEBRUARY 11
Four Things You Should Continually Commit to the Lord Luke 23:46 (NKJV)

1. YOUR WAY TO THE LORD
- ☐ Psalm 37:5

I need to commit my way to the Lord because:

a. The way is a difficult way
- ☐ Matthew 7:13-14

f. I have never been this way before
- ☐ Joshua 3:4

g. He knows the way
- ☐ Psalm 32:8
- ☐ Job 23:10

h. His way is higher than my way
- ☐ Isaiah 55:9

i. His way is the right way
- ☐ Proverbs 14:12
- ☐ Proverbs 16:25

j. His way is a more excellent way
- ☐ 1 Corinthians 12:31

k. He will show His way
- ☐ Isaiah 30:21

l. He will make a way
- ☐ Isaiah 43:16

2. YOUR WORK TO THE LORD
- ☐ Proverbs 16:3

3. YOUR WILL TO THE LORD
- ☐ Luke 22:42
- ☐ Matthew 6:10
- ☐ Hebrews 10:7-9

4. YOURSELF TO THE WORD OF THE LORD
- ☐ Deuteronomy 6:6 (NLT)
- ☐ Deuteronomy 11:18 (NLT)
- ☐ Proverbs 23:12 (NLT)

FEBRUARY 12

Biblical Aid When My Heart is Afraid
Psalm 27:1 (NKJV)

Six things to do when you are afraid:

1. PRAY
- ☐ Philippians 4:6-7
- ☐ 1 Peter 5:7

2. EXERCISE YOUR FAITH
- ☐ Matthew 8:26
- ☐ Luke 8:50

3. TRUST IN THE LORD
- ☐ Psalm 56:3-4

4. TAKE HEART
- ☐ Jeremiah 51:46

5. **REALIZE GOD IS EXTREMELY NEAR**
   - [ ] Psalm 23:4
   - [ ] Isaiah 41:10-13
   - [ ] Joshua 1:9
   - [ ] Psalm 46:1-3
   - [ ] Psalm 118:6
   - [ ] Lamentations 3:57

6. **SEEK THE LORD**
   - [ ] Psalm 34:4
   - [ ] 2 Chronicles 20:3

FEBRUARY 13

Seven Dangerous Love Affairs in Scripture (NKJV)

1. **LOVERS OF THEMSELVES**
   - [ ] 2 Timothy 3:2-5

2. **LOVERS OF MONEY**
   - [ ] 2 Timothy 3:2
   - [ ] 1 Timothy 6:10
   - [ ] Luke 16:14

3. **LOVERS OF PLEASURE**
   - [ ] 2 Timothy 3:4
   - [ ] Hebrews 11:25

4. **LOVERS OF PRAISE**
   - [ ] John 12:43

5. **LOVERS OF DARKNESS (EVIL)**
   - [ ] John 3:19
   - [ ] 1 Peter 2:9
   - [ ] Ephesians 5:8

6. **LOVERS OF THE WORLD**
   - ☐ 1 John 2:15
   - ☐ 2 Timothy 4:10
   - ☐ James 4:4
   - ☐ Ephesians 2:2

7. **LOVERS OF VANITY**
   - ☐ Psalm 4:2
   - ☐ Ecclesiastes 1:2; 2:2; 4:16; 11:10

FEBRUARY 14
Three "Let Us Love" Passages (NKJV)

1. **UNUSUAL LOVE**
   - ☐ 1 John 3:18

2. **UNCONDITIONAL LOVE**
   - ☐ 1 John 4:7

3. **UNSELFISH LOVE**
   - ☐ Hebrews 10:24

FEBRUARY 15
Four Things You Should Do Quickly (NKJV)

1. **SETTLE THINGS QUICKLY**
   - ☐ Matthew 5:25

2. **GO AND TELL OTHERS QUICKLY**
   - ☐ Luke 14:21
   - ☐ Matthew 28:7

3. **CARRY OUT TASKS QUICKLY**
   - ☐ John 9:4 (NLT)

4. **LISTEN CAREFULLY AND QUICKLY**
   - ☐ James 1:19

NOTES

FEBRUARY 16

Grace Does Not Erase the Need for Good Deeds Titus 2:7 (NKJV)

1. **GOD SEES OUR DEEDS**
   - ☐ Jonah 3:10

2. **GOOD DEEDS ARE TO BE DONE FOR GOD'S GLORY, NOT FOR OUR OWN**
   - ☐ Matthew 5:16
   - ☐ Matthew 6:1
   - ☐ Matthew 23:3-5
   - ☐ Romans 7:4
   - ☐ 1 Peter 2:12

3. **GOOD DEEDS ARE A COMPLIMENT TO GRACE, NOT A CONTRADICTION TO IT**
   - ☐ Ephesians 2:8-10
   - ☐ Acts 26:20
   - ☐ Titus 1:16
   - ☐ Titus 2:11-14

4. **FAITH WITHOUT GOOD DEADS IS DEAD**
   - ☐ James 2:14,25-26

5. **GOOD DEEDS ARE TO BE MAINTAINED**
   - ☐ Titus 3:8-14

6. **GOOD DEEDS WILL BE REWARDED IN HEAVEN**
   - ☐ Revelation 19:8

7. **GOOD DEEDS OUTLIVE US**
   - ☐ 2 Corinthians 9:9 (NLT)
   - ☐ Revelation 14:13

BEFORE YOU PUT THE SHOVEL DOWN
- ☐ Hebrews 10:24
- ☐ 1 Timothy 6:18
- ☐ Acts 9:36

FEBRUARY 17

The New Testament "Walk" Commandments (NKJV)

1. **WALK IN THE LIGHT**
   - [ ] 1 John 1:7

2. **WALK AS JESUS WALKED**
   - [ ] 1 John 2:6

3. **WALK IN THE TRUTH**
   - [ ] 2 John 1:4
   - [ ] 3 John 3-4

4. **WALK ACCORDING TO THE COMMANDMENTS**
   - [ ] 2 John 1:6

5. **WALK IN THE FEAR OF THE LORD**
   - [ ] Acts 9:31

6. **WALK IN NEWNESS OF LIFE**
   - [ ] Romans 6:4
   - [ ] Romans 13:13

7. **WALK BY FAITH**
   - [ ] 2 Corinthians 5:7

8. **WALK WORTHY**
   - [ ] Ephesians 2:10
   - [ ] Colossians 1:10
   - [ ] 1 Thessalonians 2:10-12

9. **WALK IN LOVE**
   - [ ] Ephesians 5:2

10. **WALK CAREFULLY IN WISDOM**
    - [ ] Ephesians 5:15

BEFORE YOU PUT THE SHOVEL DOWN
- [ ] Philippians 3:17

FEBRUARY 18

The Four-fold Purpose for Why Jesus Was Manifested (NKJV)

1. **THAT WE COULD BEAR WITNESS TO THE TRUTH**
   ☐ 1 John 1:1-2

2. **TO TAKE AWAY OUR SIN**
   ☐ 1 John 3:4-6

3. **TO DESTROY THE WORKS OF THE DEVIL**
   ☐ 1 John 3:8

4. **THAT WE MIGHT LIVE THROUGH HIM**
   ☐ 1 John 4:9

BEFORE YOU PUT THE SHOVEL DOWN
☐ 1 Timothy 3:16
☐ 1 Peter 1:20

FEBRUARY 19

The 15 Things "We Know" in 1 John (NKJV)

☐ 1 John 2:3
☐ 1 John 2:5
☐ 1 John 2:18
☐ 1 John 3:2
☐ 1 John 3:14
☐ 1 John 3:16
☐ 1 John 3:19
☐ 1 John 3:24
☐ 1 John 4:6
☐ 1 John 4:13
☐ 1 John 5:2
☐ 1 John 5:15
☐ 1 John 5:18
☐ 1 John 5:19
☐ 1 John 5:20

FEBRUARY 20
Five Things God Requires of Us
Micah 6:8-9 (NLT)

1. **TO DO WHAT IS RIGHT**
   - ☐ Micah 6:8

2. **TO LOVE MERCY**
   - ☐ Micah 6:8
   - ☐ Matthew 5:7

3. **TO WALK HUMBLY WITH GOD**
   - ☐ Micah 6:8
   - ☐ 2 Chronicles 7:14

4. **TO LISTEN**
   - ☐ Micah 6:9
   - ☐ John 10:27-28
   - ☐ 1 Samuel 3

5. **TO FEAR GOD**
   - ☐ Micah 6:9

FEBRUARY 21
Are You the One? *Matthew 11:1-3 (NIV)*

Jesus is:

1. **THE ONE AND ONLY SON OF GOD**
   - ☐ John 3:16

2. **THE ONE AND ONLY TRUTH**
   - ☐ John 14:6
   - ☐ Matthew 22:16
   - ☐ John 1:14,17
   - ☐ John 8:32

3. **THE ONE AND ONLY WAY**
   - ☐ John 14:6
   - ☐ Matthew 7:13-14

4. **THE ONE AND ONLY NAME BY WHICH WE MAY BE SAVED**
   - ☐ Acts 4:12

FEBRUARY 22

The Battle *2 Corinthians 7:5 (NLT)*

Some important things you need to know about the battle:

1. **WE ARE IN A BATTLE**
   - ☐ 2 Corinthians 2:11
   - ☐ 1 Peter 5:8

2. **THE BATTLE IS BIGGER THAN WE ARE**
   - ☐ Ephesians 6:12-13

3. **THE BATTLE IS THE LORD'S, NOT OURS**
   - ☐ 2 Chronicles 20:15
   - ☐ Exodus 14:14
   - ☐ 1 Samuel 17:47

4. **THE LORD WILL GO BEFORE US INTO THE BATTLE**
   - ☐ Exodus 23:23
   - ☐ 1 Chronicles 14:15
   - ☐ Isaiah 52:12

5. **THE LORD WILL BE WITH US THROUGH THE BATTLE**
   - ☐ Deuteronomy 20:1
   - ☐ 2 Chronicles 20:17
   - ☐ 2 Chronicles 32:8
   - ☐ Zechariah 10:5

NOTES

6. **GOD WILL STRENGTHEN US IN THE BATTLE**
   - [ ] 2 Samuel 22:40
   - [ ] Psalm 18:39
   - [ ] Hebrews 11:33-34

7. **WITH GOD ON OUR SIDE, WE WILL WIN THE BATTLE**
   - [ ] 1 Corinthians 15:57
   - [ ] Romans 8:35-37
   - [ ] 1 John 2:13
   - [ ] 1 John 5:4-5

BEFORE YOU PUT THE SHOVEL DOWN
   - [ ] 1 Timothy 6:12
   - [ ] 2 Timothy 4:7
   - [ ] Psalm 24:8
   - [ ] 1 Timothy 1:18

DON'T LET THE BATTLE RATTLE YOU.

FEBRUARY 23

Six Giving Requirements (NKJV)

1. **GIVE PRIVATELY**
   - [ ] Matthew 6:1-4

2. **GIVE FAITHFULLY**
   - [ ] 1 Corinthians 4:2

3. **GIVE SYSTEMATICALLY**
   - [ ] 1 Corinthians 16:2

4. **GIVE SACRIFICIALLY**
   - [ ] 2 Corinthians 8:2
   - [ ] Luke 21:3-4

5. **GIVE UNSPARINGLY**
   - [ ] 2 Corinthians 9:6

6. **GIVE CHEERFULLY**
   - [ ] 2 Corinthians 9:7

FEBRUARY 24

I Am Resolved (NIV)

1. **LIKE JEHOSHAPHAT, TO INQUIRE OF THE LORD**
   - ☐ 2 Chronicles 20:3

2. **LIKE DAVID, TO NOT SIN**
   - ☐ Psalm 17:3
   - ☐ Psalm 119:11

3. **LIKE DANIEL, TO NOT DEFILE HIMSELF**
   - ☐ Daniel 1:8
   - ☐ Psalm 106:39

4. **LIKE PAUL, TO KNOW CHRIST**
   - ☐ 1 Corinthians 2:2
   - ☐ Philippians 3:10

FEBRUARY 25

The Five Problems of Not Inquiring of the Lord (NKJV)

1. **IT GETS ME INTO DIFFICULTY I CANNOT GET OUT OF**
   - ☐ Joshua 9:14

2. **IT TAKES ME DOWN PATHS OF DESTRUCTION**
   - ☐ 1 Chronicles 10:13-14
   - ☐ Zephaniah 1:4-6

3. **IT BECOMES HABIT FORMING**
   - ☐ 1 Chronicles 13:3

4. **IT STRAINS MY RELATIONSHIP WITH GOD**
   - ☐ 1 Chronicles 15:13-15

5. **IT KEEPS ME FROM PROSPERING**
   ☐ Jeremiah 10:21

BEFORE YOU PUT THE SHOVEL DOWN
☐ Isaiah 30:1-2

FEBRUARY 26
Three Practices of Jesus That Could Change Your Life (NLT)

1. **I ONLY DO WHAT I SEE THE FATHER DOING**
   ☐ John 5:19
   ☐ John 6:38

2. **I ONLY SAY WHAT I HAVE HEARD FROM THE FATHER**
   ☐ John 7:16
   ☐ John 8:26
   ☐ John 12:49

3. **I ONLY GO WHERE THE FATHER SENDS ME**
   ☐ John 4:34
   ☐ John 5:30
   ☐ John 17:18
   ☐ John 20:21

FEBRUARY 27
Elements of a Quality Quiet Time
Acts 4:13 (NKJV)

1. **OFTEN**
   ☐ Luke 5:16
   ☐ John 18:2

2. **EARLY**
   - [ ] Mark 1:35
   - [ ] 1 Samuel 1:19
   - [ ] Psalm 5:3
   - [ ] Psalm 63:1
   - [ ] Psalm 90:14
   - [ ] Job 1:5

3. **SOLITARY PLACE**
   - [ ] Mark 1:35
   - [ ] Mark 6:31
   - [ ] Luke 22:41

4. **PRAYER AND PRAISE**
   - [ ] Luke 5:16
   - [ ] Mark 1:35

5. **READING SCRIPTURE**
   - [ ] 2 Timothy 2:15
   - [ ] 2 Timothy 3:16-17

6. **MEDITATION AND REFLECTION**
   - [ ] Psalm 1:2
   - [ ] Psalm 4:4
   - [ ] Psalm 63:6
   - [ ] Joshua 1:8-9

7. **JOURNALING**
   - [ ] Revelation 1:11
   - [ ] Isaiah 30:8
   - [ ] Habakkuk 2:2
   - [ ] Jeremiah 30:2

8. **ACTION**
   - [ ] James 1:22-25
   - [ ] Philippians 4:9
   - [ ] Matthew 7:24-26

FEBRUARY 28

The Secret to Seeking God
Acts 17:26-31 (NKJV)

Starting to Dig
- ☐ Psalm 14:2
- ☐ Psalm 53:2
- ☐ Romans 3:11
- ☐ 2 Chronicles 16:12
- ☐ Isaiah 31:1

1. **WE ARE TO SEEK GOD EARLY IN THE MORNING**
   - ☐ Psalm 63:1

2. **WE ARE TO PREPARE OUR HEART TO SEEK THE LORD**
   - ☐ 2 Chronicles 12:14
   - ☐ Psalm 24:3-6
   - ☐ Ezra 7:10

3. **WE ARE TO SEEK GOD WHILE HE MAY BE FOUND**
   - ☐ Isaiah 55:6-7

4. **WE ARE TO SEEK FIRST THE KINGDOM OF GOD**
   - ☐ Matthew 6:31-33
   - ☐ Colossians 3:1-2

5. **WE ARE TO KEEP ON SEEKING GOD**
   - ☐ Matthew 7:7-8
   - ☐ Psalm 105:4
   - ☐ 1 Chronicles 16:11

NOTES

6. WE WILL FIND HIM WHEN WE SEEK GOD WITH ALL OUR HEART AND SOUL

- [ ] Deuteronomy 4:29
- [ ] Jeremiah 29:13
- [ ] Psalm 119:2
- [ ] 1 Chronicles 28:9
- [ ] 2 Chronicles 22:9
- [ ] 2 Chronicles 31:21
- [ ] Hebrews 11:6
- [ ] Proverbs 8:17
- [ ] Proverbs 2:4

7. WE ARE TO SEEK THE LORD WITH HUMILITY

- [ ] Zephaniah 2:3
- [ ] Psalm 10:4
- [ ] 2 Chronicles 33:12
- [ ] 2 Chronicles 7:14

BEFORE YOU PUT THE SHOVEL DOWN

- [ ] Psalm 34:10
- [ ] Lamentations 3:25
- [ ] 1 Chronicles 22:19
- [ ] Job 5:8

FEBRUARY 29

Eight Things the Bible Challenges Us to Do Wholeheartedly

Jeremiah 24:7 (NLT)

1. SEEK GOD WHOLEHEARTEDLY

- [ ] 2 Chronicles 31:21
- [ ] Jeremiah 29:13

2. FOLLOW WHOLEHEARTEDLY

- [ ] Joshua 14:8-14
- [ ] Numbers 14:24 (NIV)
- [ ] Numbers 32:11-12 (NIV)
- [ ] Deuteronomy 1:36 (NIV)
- [ ] Psalm 119:80 (NIV)

3. **GIVE WHOLEHEARTEDLY**
   - ☐ 1 Chronicles 29:9

4. **WALK BEFORE GOD WHOLEHEARTEDLY**
   - ☐ 2 Chronicles 6:14
   - ☐ 1 Kings 8:23

5. **WORK WHOLEHEARTEDLY**
   - ☐ 2 Chronicles 31:21

6. **OBEY WHOLEHEARTEDLY**
   - ☐ Romans 6:17
   - ☐ Numbers 32:11
   - ☐ Deuteronomy 6:6
   - ☐ Deuteronomy 11:18
   - ☐ Deuteronomy 26:16

7. **SERVE WHOLEHEARTEDLY**
   - ☐ Ephesians 6:7 (NIV)
   - ☐ 1 Chronicles 28:9
   - ☐ Joshua 24:14

8. **AGREE WITH EACH OTHER WHOLEHEARTEDLY**
   - ☐ Philippians 2:2

NOTES

MARCH

MARCH 1

What the Bible Has to Say About Itself (NKJV)

1. **IT IS INSPIRED**
   - ☐ 2 Timothy 3:16
   - ☐ 2 Peter 1:20-21

2. **IT IS PROFITABLE**
   - ☐ 2 Timothy 3:16

3. **IT IS ENDURING**
   - ☐ 1 Peter 1:25
   - ☐ Matthew 24:35
   - ☐ Isaiah 40:8
   - ☐ Psalm 119:89

4. **IT IS LIVING**
   - ☐ Hebrews 4:12

5. **IT WILL BE FULFILLED**
   - ☐ Matthew 5:18

6. **IT IS A WEAPON**
   - ☐ Ephesians 6:17
   - ☐ Hebrews 4:12

7. **IT IS TRUTH**
   - ☐ John 17:17

8. **IT IS AN ENCOURAGEMENT**
   - ☐ Romans 15:4

9. **IT IS COMPLETE**
   - ☐ Revelation 22:19

10. **IT WILL BUILD YOU UP**
    - ☐ Acts 20:32

NOTES

MARCH 2

11 Paradoxes in the New Testament:
[Part 1] (NIV)

1. **THE KEY TO BEING FIRST IS BEING LAST**
   - ☐ Matthew 19:30
   - ☐ Matthew 20:16

2. **THE KEY TO LIVING IS DYING**
   - ☐ 2 Corinthians 6:3-10
   - ☐ Galatians 2:20
   - ☐ John 12:24

3. **THE KEY TO BEING THE GREATEST IS BECOMING THE LEAST**
   - ☐ Matthew 20:26
   - ☐ Matthew 23:11

4. **THE KEY TO BEING EXALTED IS BEING HUMBLE**
   - ☐ James 4:6-10
   - ☐ Matthew 23:12
   - ☐ Philippians 2:5-9

5. **THE KEY TO RECEIVING IS GIVING**
   - ☐ Luke 6:38
   - ☐ Proverbs 11:24-25
   - ☐ Ecclesiastes 11:1

6. **THE KEY TO BEING RICH IS BECOMING POOR**
   - ☐ 2 Corinthians 6:10
   - ☐ 2 Corinthians 8:9
   - ☐ James 2:5

MARCH 3

11 Paradoxes in the New Testament:
[Part 2] (NIV)

1. **THE KEY TO MATURITY IS BECOMING CHILDLIKE**
   - ☐ Matthew 18:1-4

2. **THE KEY TO FINDING YOUR LIFE IS LOSING IT**
   - ☐ Matthew 10:39
   - ☐ John 12:25
   - ☐ Philippians 3:8

3. **THE KEY TO BEING FREE IS BECOMING A SLAVE**
   - ☐ 1 Corinthians 9:19

4. **THE KEY TO BEING WISE IS BECOMING A FOOL**
   - ☐ 1 Corinthians 1:18-27
   - ☐ 1 Corinthians 3:18
   - ☐ 1 Corinthians 4:10

5. **THE KEY TO BEING STRONG IS BEING MADE WEAK**
   - ☐ 2 Corinthians 12:9-10
   - ☐ Hebrews 11:32-34
   - ☐ 1 Corinthians 1:27

MARCH 4

Four Proofs We Are Still Controlled By the Sinful Nature *1 Corinthians 3:1-4 [NLT]*

1. **BEING JEALOUS OF OTHERS**
   - ☐ 1 Corinthians 3:3
   - ☐ James 3:14-16
   - ☐ Galatians 5:19-20

2. QUARRELLING WITH EACH OTHER
- ☐ 1 Corinthians 3:3
- ☐ Proverbs 17:14,19
- ☐ Proverbs 26:20
- ☐ Romans 1:29
- ☐ Romans 13:13
- ☐ 1 Corinthians 1:11
- ☐ Galatians 5:20
- ☐ James 4:1-2

3. BEING AT ODDS WITH OTHERS
- ☐ 1 Corinthians 3:3 (NKJV)
- ☐ 1 Corinthians 1:10
- ☐ 1 Corinthians 11:18

4. LIVING LIKE THE WORLD
- ☐ 1 Corinthians 3:3
- ☐ Psalm 118:8-9

MARCH 5
When Making a Decision [NKJV]

Ask yourself these questions:

1. IS IT HARMFUL TO ME OR ANOTHER?
- ☐ Philippians 4:8-9

2. WILL IT BE A HINDRANCE TO ME OR SOMEONE ELSE?
- ☐ Romans 14:13-22

3. WILL IT BE HELPFUL TO MY SPIRITUAL JOURNEY?
- ☐ 2 Peter 1:5-11
- ☐ 2 Peter 3:17-18

4. WILL IT BRING GOD GLORY?
- ☐ 1 Thessalonians 4:1
- ☐ 2 Corinthians 5:9-10
- ☐ Colossians 1:10

5. **IS IT HIGHLIGHTED WITHIN GOD'S WORD?**
   - ☐ Colossians 3:16-17
   - ☐ Psalm 119:11

6. **DO I HAVE A HESITATION IN DOING IT?**
   - ☐ Psalm 37:23

7. **IS MY HEART AND SPIRIT SETTLED?**
   - ☐ Philippians 4:6-7

8. **WOULD ANY HURDLES HALT MY DECISION?**
   - ☐ Philippians 4:10
   - ☐ Revelation 3:7-8

9. **IS THERE ANY HANDWRITING ON THE WALL? PROVIDENTIAL EVENTS?**
   - ☐ John 20:30-31

10. **HAVE I SOUGHT GOD'S WISDOM AND THE COUNSEL OF MEN?**
    - ☐ James 1:5

11. **IS IT IN ACCORDANCE WITH GOD'S HIGH STANDARD OF HOLY LIVING?**
    - ☐ 1 Peter 1:15

MARCH 6
What Does It Profit? (NKJV)

1. **WHAT IS THE PROFIT OF ALL THE WORK?**
   - ☐ Ecclesiastes 1:3
   - ☐ Ecclesiastes 3:9
   - ☐ Ecclesiastes 5:11,16

2. **WHAT DOES IT PROFIT IF YOU GAIN THE WHOLE WORLD AND LOSE YOUR OWN SOUL?**
   - ☐ Matthew 16:26
   - ☐ Mark 8:36

3. **WHAT DOES IT PROFIT IF YOU HAVE FAITH AND NOT WORKS?**
   - ☐ James 2:14,16

MARCH 7

Satan and His Schemes: [Part 1]
2 Corinthians 2:11 (NIV)

Satan's three primary objectives:

1. **DISRUPT AND DIVERT**
   - ☐ 1 Timothy 5:15

2. **DECEIVE**
   - ☐ Genesis 3:13
   - ☐ 2 Corinthians 11:3

3. **DIVIDE AND DESTROY**
   - ☐ John 10:10
   - ☐ 1 Peter 5:8

Look at Satan's schemes:

1. **SATAN SCHEMES TO TRAP THE BELIEVER**
   - ☐ 1 Timothy 3:6-7
   - ☐ 2 Timothy 2:26
   - ☐ 1 Timothy 6:9

2. **SATAN SCHEMES TO HINDER THE WORK OF GOD AND THE WAY OF GOD'S PEOPLE**
   - ☐ 1 Thessalonians 2:18
   - ☐ 1 Thessalonians 3:5

3. **SATAN SCHEMES TO UNDERMINE GOD'S ACTIVITY**
   - ☐ Mark 4:15

4. **SATAN SCHEMES TO MISREPRESENT THE TRUTH OF SCRIPTURE**
   - ☐ Matthew 4:6

5. **SATAN SCHEMES TO TEMPT INTO SIN**
   - ☐ Matthew 4:1-3
   - ☐ 1 Thessalonians 3:5
   - ☐ 1 Corinthians 10:13

MARCH 8

Satan and His Schemes: [Part 2] (NIV)

1. **SATAN SCHEMES TO BLIND THE HEARTS OF MEN AND WOMEN**
   - ☐ 2 Corinthians 4:3-4

2. **SATAN SCHEMES TO INFLICT PHYSICAL TORMENT ON BELIEVERS**
   - ☐ 2 Corinthians 12:7
   - ☐ Luke 13:16

3. **SATAN SCHEMES TO INSTIGATE EVIL**
   - ☐ John 13:2,27

4. **SATAN SCHEMES TO DECEIVE**
   - ☐ Revelation 12:9
   - ☐ Acts 13:8-11
   - ☐ 2 Thessalonians 2:9
   - ☐ 2 Corinthians 11:13-14

5. **SATAN SCHEMES THROUGH HIS LIES**
   - ☐ John 8:44

6. **SATAN SCHEMES TO QUESTION GOD AND CREATE DOUBTS IN OTHERS**
   - ☐ Genesis 3:1
   - ☐ Luke 4:3

MARCH 9
The Three Dangers of Anxiety (NKJV)

1. **IT CAUSES HARM**
   - ☐ Psalm 37:8

2. **IT CAUSES DEPRESSION**
   - ☐ Proverbs 12:25
   - ☐ Luke 21:34

3. **IT CAUSES INNER TURMOIL**
   - ☐ Job 20:2

BEFORE YOU PUT THE SHOVEL DOWN
   - ☐ Philippians 4:4-13

MARCH 10
Seven Ways God May Use a Test
1 Peter 4:12-16 (NASB)

1. **PROBE**
   - ☐ Deuteronomy 8:2
   - ☐ Deuteronomy 13:3
   - ☐ 2 Chronicles 32:31

2. **PROVE SOMETHING OR SOMEONE**
   - ☐ Genesis 22:1
   - ☐ Genesis 22:12
   - ☐ Hebrews 11:17
   - ☐ John 6:6

3. **PRUNE**
   - ☐ Judges 7:4
   - ☐ John 15
   - ☐ Luke 8:13 (NIV)
   - ☐ Hebrews 3:8 (NIV)

4. **PREPARE**
   - ☐ Psalm 105:19 (NLT)
   - ☐ Jeremiah 12:3 (NLT)

NOTES

5. **PRODUCE SOMETHING VALUABLE**
   - ☐ 2 Corinthians 8:2 (NLT)
   - ☐ James 1:3,12 (NLT)

6. **PURIFY**
   - ☐ Psalm 66:10
   - ☐ 1 Peter 1:7
   - ☐ Zechariah 13:9
   - ☐ Job 23:10

7. **PREVENT**
   - ☐ Exodus 20:20

BEFORE YOU PUT THE SHOVEL DOWN
- ☐ Romans 16:10 (NIV)

MARCH 11
Four Keys to Spiritual Growth
Matthew 13 (NIV)

1. **HEAR THE WORD**
   - ☐ Matthew 13:19a
   - ☐ Romans 10:17

2. **RECEIVE THE WORD**
   - ☐ Matthew 13:20-23
   - ☐ Acts 11:1
   - ☐ 1 Thessalonians 2:13

3. **UNDERSTAND THE WORD**
   - ☐ Matthew 13:19b,23

4. **PUT THE WORD INTO PRACTICE**
   - ☐ Matthew 7:24-26
   - ☐ Luke 8:21

MARCH 12
Be of Good Cheer (NKJV)

Five places where Jesus gives us something to cheer about:

1. **BE OF GOOD CHEER—YOUR SINS ARE FORGIVEN**
   - ☐ Matthew 9:2

2. **BE OF GOOD CHEER—YOUR FAITH HAS MADE YOU WELL**
   - ☐ Matthew 9:22

3. **BE OF GOOD CHEER—IT IS I, DO NOT BE AFRAID**
   - ☐ Matthew 14:27

4. **BE OF GOOD CHEER—RISE, HE IS CALLING YOU**
   - ☐ Mark 10:49

5. **BE OF GOOD CHEER—I HAVE OVERCOME**
   - ☐ John 16:33

MARCH 13
Three Conclusions About Comfort

2 Corinthians 1:1-7 (NIV)

1. **GOD IS THE GOD OF ALL COMFORT**
   - ☐ 2 Corinthians 1:3
   - ☐ Isaiah 51:12
   - ☐ Isaiah 52:9

NOTES

2. **WHO COMFORTS US IN ALL OUR TROUBLES**
   - ☐ 2 Corinthians 1:4
   - ☐ Isaiah 49:13
   - ☐ Isaiah 66:13
   - ☐ Psalm 119:50 (NLT)

3. **SO WE CAN COMFORT THOSE IN ANY TROUBLE**
   - ☐ 2 Corinthians 1:4b
   - ☐ Isaiah 40:1
   - ☐ 2 Corinthians 1:6-7

MARCH 14
Comfort Comes From (NKJV)

1. **GOD THE FATHER**
   - ☐ 2 Corinthians 1:3

2. **GOD THE SON** (Jesus)
   - ☐ 2 Corinthians 1:5

3. **GOD THE HOLY SPIRIT**
   - ☐ John 14:26
   - ☐ John 15:26
   - ☐ John 16:7

4. **GOD'S WORD**
   - ☐ Romans 15:4

MARCH 15

Three Critical Turns in Life's Journey *Isaiah 55:6-9 (NIV)*

2. **TURN TO GOD** (road called: salvation)
   - ☐ Isaiah 45:22
   - ☐ Isaiah 55:7
   - ☐ Matthew 3:2
   - ☐ Matthew 4:17
   - ☐ Acts 3:19

3. **TURN FROM SIN** (road called: Sanctification)
   - ☐ Go sin no more:
     - ☐ John 5:14
     - ☐ John 8:11 (KJV)
   - ☐ Romans 6:1-2
   - ☐ 1 John 2:1
   - ☐ 2 Timothy 2:19

4. **TURN OVER EVERYTHING TO CHRIST** (road called: surrender)
   - ☐ Acts 14:15
   - ☐ Jonah 2:8

MARCH 16

Three Dangerous Turns Once You've Turned to God (NKJV)

1. **TURNING ASIDE FROM THE TRUTH**
   - ☐ 1 Timothy 1:5-7
   - ☐ 1 Timothy 5:14-15
   - ☐ 2 Timothy 4:4

NOTES

2. **TURNING BACK IN OUR HEARTS**
   - ☐ Acts 7:39
   - ☐ Luke 9:62

3. **TURNING AWAY TO A DIFFERENT GOSPEL**
   - ☐ Galatians 1:6

MARCH 17
Three Inappropriate Approaches to Sin (NIV)

1. **THE ACT OF SIN**
   - ☐ Galatians 5:19
   - ☐ Psalm 106:6

2. **THE ATTITUDE OF SIN**
   - ☐ Matthew 5:27-30

3. **THE APPROVAL OF SIN**
   - ☐ Acts 8:1
   - ☐ Acts 22:20
   - ☐ Romans 14:22

MARCH 18
The Three Little Bears in Scripture (NKJV)

1. **BEAR WITH THE WEAK AND ONE ANOTHER'S BURDENS**
   - ☐ Romans 15:1
   - ☐ Galatians 6:2
   - ☐ Colossians 3:13

2. **BEAR MUCH FRUIT**
   - ☐ John 15:1-5

3. **BEAR YOUR OWN LOAD**
   - ☐ Galatians 6:2-5

MARCH 19

Three Keys to Prayer *Psalm 5:1-3 (NLT)*

1. EACH MORNING
- ☐ Psalm 88:13 (NKJV)
- ☐ Psalm 143:8
- ☐ Psalm 90:14
- ☐ Psalm 119:147
- ☐ Mark 1:35

2. I BRING MY REQUESTS TO YOU
- ☐ Philippians 4:6-7 (NKJV)
- ☐ 1 Peter 5:6-7 (NKJV)

3. AND WAIT EXPECTANTLY
- ☐ James 5:16
- ☐ Luke 2:38

MARCH 20

Five Things the Bible Tells Us to Flee From (NIV)

1. SEXUAL IMMORALITY
- ☐ 1 Corinthians 6:18

2. IDOLATRY
- ☐ 1 Corinthians 10:14

3. LOVE OF MONEY
- ☐ 1 Timothy 6:11

4. EVIL DESIRES
- ☐ 2 Timothy 2:22

5. THE DEVIL
- ☐ James 4:7

NOTES

MARCH 21
Three Commands for Christians Regarding the World (NKJV)

1. **DO NOT LOVE THE WORLD**
   - ☐ 1 John 2:15-16
   - ☐ 2 Timothy 4:10
   - ☐ James 1:27

2. **DO NOT CONFORM TO THE WORLD**
   - ☐ Romans 12:2

3. **DO NOT BE OF THE WORLD**
   - ☐ John 8:23
   - ☐ John 15:18-19
   - ☐ John 17:14-17

MARCH 22
Four Things the Bible Teaches We Must Work At (NLT)

1. **TELLING OTHERS ABOUT THE GOOD NEWS**
   - ☐ 2 Timothy 4:5

2. **FULLY CARRYING OUT THE MINISTRY GOD GAVE US**
   - ☐ 2 Timothy 4:5

3. **LIVING AT PEACE WITH EVERYONE**
   - ☐ Hebrews 12:14
   - ☐ Romans 12:18 (NKJV)

4. **LIVING A HOLY LIFE**
   - ☐ Hebrews 12:14

MARCH 23
Who Then Can Be Saved?
Matthew 19:25 (NKJV)

1. **THOSE WHO BELIEVE**
   - ☐ Mark 16:16
   - ☐ John 3:16
   - ☐ Luke 8:12
   - ☐ Acts 16:30-31
   - ☐ Romans 10:9-10

2. **THOSE WHO CALL ON THE NAME OF THE LORD**
   - ☐ Acts 2:21
   - ☐ Romans 10:13

3. **THOSE WHO ENTER THE EXPERIENCE OF SALVATION**
   - ☐ John 10:9
   - ☐ Luke 13:22-26

4. **THOSE WHO RECEIVE THIS GIFT OF GRACE BY FAITH**
   - ☐ Ephesians 2:8
   - ☐ 2 Timothy 1:9

5. **THOSE WHO HAVE BEEN JUSTIFIED BY HIS BLOOD**
   - ☐ Romans 5:9

6. **THOSE WHO ENDURE TO THE END**
   - ☐ Matthew 10:22
   - ☐ 1 Corinthians 15:2

NOTES

MARCH 24
Three Times God's Voice Was Heard Regarding His Son (NKJV)

1. **AT JESUS' BAPTISM**
   - ☐ Matthew 3:16-17
   - ☐ Mark 1:11
   - ☐ Luke 3:21-22

2. **AT THE MOUNT OF TRANSFIGURATION**
   - ☐ Matthew 17:5
   - ☐ Mark 9:7
   - ☐ Luke 9:35-36
   - ☐ 2 Peter 1:17-18

3. **AS HE PREPARED TO GO TO THE CROSS**
   - ☐ John 12:28

MARCH 25
The End of the World is Coming Soon Therefore 1 Peter 4:7-11 (NLT)

We tend to focus on <u>when</u> He is coming back and not on <u>what</u> we need to be doing.

1. **BE EARNEST AND DISCIPLINED IN YOUR PRAYERS**
   - ☐ 1 Peter 4:7
   - ☐ Colossians 4:2
   - ☐ Mark 14:37-38
   - ☐ Romans 12:12
   - ☐ Ephesians 6:18

2. **CONTINUALLY SHOW DEEP LOVE FOR EACH OTHER**
   - ☐ 1 Peter 4:8
   - ☐ 1 Peter 1:22
   - ☐ 1 Thessalonians 3:12
   - ☐ Proverbs 10:12
   - ☐ Colossians 3:14
   - ☐ James 5:20

3. **CHEERFULLY SHARE**
   - ☐ 1 Peter 4:9
   - ☐ Acts 2:42-47

4. **USE YOUR GIFTS**
   - ☐ 1 Peter 4:10

5. **MAKE EVERY EFFORT TO LIVE PEACEFUL, PURE AND BLAMELESS IN HIS SIGHT**
   - ☐ 2 Peter 3:14

MARCH 26

Let Us (NKJV)

1. **FEAR**
   - ☐ Hebrews 4:1

2. **BE DILIGENT**
   - ☐ Hebrews 4:11

3. **HOLD FAST TO OUR CONFESSION**
   - ☐ Hebrews 4:14

4. **COME BOLDLY TO THE THRONE OF GRACE**
   - ☐ Hebrews 4:16

5. **GO ON TO PERFECTION**
   - ☐ Hebrews 6:1

6. **DRAW NEAR**
   - ☐ Hebrews 10:22

7. **HOLD FAST TO HOPE**
   - ☐ Hebrews 10:23

8. **CONSIDER ONE ANOTHER**
   - ☐ Hebrews 10:24

9. **LAY ASIDE EVERY WEIGHT**
   - ☐ Hebrews 12:1

10. **RUN WITH ENDURANCE**
    - ☐ Hebrews 12:1-2

11. **HAVE GRACE TO SERVE GOD**
    - ☐ Hebrews 12:28

12. **SHARE IN HIS SUFFERINGS**
    - ☐ Hebrews 13:13

13. **CONTINUALLY OFFER THE SACRIFICE OF PRAISE**
    - ☐ Hebrews 13:15

MARCH 27
We Are to Acknowledge (NIV)

1. **SIN**
   - ☐ Psalm 51:3 (NKJV)
   - ☐ Psalm 32:5
   - ☐ Isaiah 59:12
   - ☐ Jeremiah 3:13
   - ☐ Jeremiah 9:3
   - ☐ Jeremiah 14:20

2. **HIM**
   - ☐ Proverbs 3:5-6
   - ☐ Jeremiah 9:6
   - ☐ Hosea 8:2
   - ☐ 1 Chronicles 28:9
   - ☐ Romans 14:11
   - ☐ Philippians 2:11
   - ☐ 1 John 2:23

3. **HIS BLESSINGS**
   - [ ] Isaiah 61:9

4. **GOD BEFORE OTHERS**
   - [ ] Matthew 10:32
   - [ ] Luke 12:8

5. **THOSE WHO WORK HARD**
   - [ ] 1 Thessalonians 5:12

MARCH 28

The Autopsy of Sin *James 1:14-15 (NKJV)*

1. **WE ARE ENTICED**
   - [ ] James 1:14-15

2. **DESIRE IS CONCEIVED**
   - [ ] James 1:14-15

3. **WE ARE DRAWN AWAY**
   - [ ] James 1:14-15

4. **WE SIN**
   - [ ] James 1:14-15

5. **WHEN FULL GROWN, IT PRODUCES DEATH**
   - [ ] James 1:14-15

MARCH 29

The Plot to Kill Jesus: [Part 1]
Matthew 26:1-67 (NKJV)

This was NOT the first plot to kill Jesus. At least five other documented attempts to kill Jesus are recorded in Scripture:

    1. Matthew 2:13-20
    2. Matthew 4:5-6
    3. Luke 4:16-30
    4. John 8:31;57-59
    5. John 10:22;31-39

We need to ask a few key questions with every crime investigation:

1. WHO DID IT?
- [ ] Matthew 27:20-26

2. HOW DID THEY DO IT?
- [ ] They sought evidence against Him, but they could not find any *(Matthew 26:60-61)*
- [ ] They sought false testimony *(Matthew 26:59-61)*
- [ ] Trickery *(Isaiah 25:11; Matthew 26:4; Ephesians 4:14)*

3. WHY DID THEY DO IT?
- [ ] Matthew 27:18

MARCH 30

The Plot to Kill Jesus: [Part 2] (NKJV)

Three primary motives are revealed as to why the Jews sought to kill Jesus:

1. **ENVY**
   - ☐ Matthew 27:18
   - ☐ John 11:45-53

2. **FEAR**
   - ☐ Mark 11:18
   - ☐ Matthew 21:46
   - ☐ Matthew 10:28

3. **HATE**
   - ☐ Luke 19:14
   - ☐ Luke 6:11
   - ☐ John 7:7
   - ☐ John 15:18-25

They hated him because:
   a. He called them out *(Matthew 3:7; Matthew 12:34; Matthew 23:33)*
   b. He claimed to be God *(John 5:16-18; John 7:30-32; John 8:58-59; John 10:22-40)*
   c. He broke their traditions *(Matthew 12:1-14)*
   d. He healed on the Sabbath *(Luke 13:10-16)*
   e. He spent time with sinners *(Matthew 9:11; Matthew 11:19; Mark 2:15)*
   f. He spoke of salvation for those beyond the Jewish nation *(Luke 4:14-30; 1 Thessalonians 2:14-15)*

See why these motivations are so dangerous:
   - ☐ Galatians 5:19-21
   - ☐ Mark 7:20-23

MARCH 31

Six Dangerous Things to Refuse
Genesis 4:7 (NLT)

You lose when you refuse:

1. **TO FORGIVE**
   ☐ Matthew 6:15

2. **TO REPENT**
   ☐ Matthew 12:41

3. **TO LISTEN**
   ☐ Matthew 12:42

4. **TO BELIEVE**
   ☐ Matthew 21:32

5. **TURN FROM SIN**
   ☐ Romans 2:5

6. **TO OBEY GOD'S STANDARDS**
   ☐ 1 Thessalonians 4:8

APRIL

APRIL 1
Five Types of Fools in Scripture
Ephesians 5:15 (NKJV)

1. **THE ERODED FOOL**
   ☐ Matthew 7:26-27

2. **THE EMPTY FOOL**
   ☐ Matthew 25:1-13

3. **THE EAGER FOOL**
   ☐ Luke 12:13-21

4. **THE EFFORT FOOL**
   ☐ Galatians 3:1-14

5. **THE FOOL FOR CHRIST**
   ☐ 1 Corinthians 4:10

APRIL 2
Four Things We Are Commanded to Do Without Doubting *Matthew 14:31 (NKJV)*

1. **BELIEVE**
   ☐ Matthew 21:21

2. **PRAY**
   ☐ 1 Timothy 2:8

3. **OBEY**
   ☐ Acts 10:20
   ☐ Acts 11:12

4. **ASK**
   ☐ James 1:6

APRIL 3
Seven Things God Doesn't Know
1 John 3:20 (NLT)

1. **ANY SIN HIDDEN FROM HIS SIGHT**
   - ☐ Hebrews 4:13
   - ☐ Luke 8:17
   - ☐ Psalm 44:21

2. **ANYONE WHO IS NOT THE OBJECT OF HIS LOVE OR THE OUTPOURING OF HIS GRACE**
   - ☐ John 3:16
   - ☐ Romans 5:8

3. **ANYONE WHO CAN SAVE THEMSELVES AND THEREFORE DOESN'T NEED A SAVIOR**
   - ☐ Romans 3:10
   - ☐ Romans 3:23
   - ☐ Acts 4:12
   - ☐ John 14:6

4. **ANY SIN HE CANNOT FORGIVE OR ANY SINNER TOO FAR FROM TRANSFORMATION** (if we confess)
   - ☐ 1 John 1:9
   - ☐ Hebrews 7:25
   - ☐ Isaiah 1:18
   - ☐ Isaiah 59:1

5. **ANY CIRCUMSTANCE TOO DIFFICULT FOR HIM OR BEYOND HIS CONTROL**
   - ☐ Genesis 18:14
   - ☐ Jeremiah 32:17
   - ☐ Jeremiah 32:27
   - ☐ Matthew 19:26

6. **ANYONE OR ANYWHERE HE DOESN'T DESIRE FOR THE MESSAGE OF THE GOSPEL TO GO**
   - ☐ 1 John 2:2
   - ☐ Mark 16:15
   - ☐ 2 Peter 3:9

7. **ANY BETTER TIME THAN NOW TO RESPOND TO HIS INVITATION**
   - ☐ 2 Corinthians 6:2
   - ☐ Hebrews 3:7,15; 4:7
   - ☐ Isaiah 55:6
   - ☐ Revelation 3:20

APRIL 4

Seven Things We Must Learn (NIV)

1. **FOLLOW THE COMMANDS OF GOD**
   - ☐ Deuteronomy 5:1-22

2. **REVERE THE LORD**
   - ☐ Deuteronomy 4:10
   - ☐ Deuteronomy 14:23

3. **FEAR THE LORD**
   - ☐ Deuteronomy 31:12-13

4. **DO WHAT IS RIGHT**
   - ☐ Titus 3:14
   - ☐ Isaiah 1:17

5. **CONTROL OUR OWN BODY**
   - ☐ 1 Thessalonians 4:3-4

6. **BE CONTENT**
   - ☐ Philippians 4:11-12

7. **REST IN CHRIST**
   - ☐ Matthew 11:29

APRIL 5

The Three Crosses at Calvary
Mark 15:27, Luke 23:32-43 (NKJV)

1. **THE CROSS OF REDEMPTION**
   - ☐ Luke 23:34
   - ☐ Titus 2:14
   - ☐ Romans 3:24
   - ☐ 1 Corinthians 1:30
   - ☐ Hebrews 9:12
   - ☐ Ephesians 1:7

2. **THE CROSS OF REJECTION**
   - ☐ Luke 23:39
   - ☐ Mark 8:31
   - ☐ Hebrews 2:3
   - ☐ Luke 10:16
   - ☐ John 1:11
   - ☐ Luke 17:25

3. **THE CROSS OF RECEPTION**
   - ☐ Luke 23:40-43
   - ☐ Four important aspects of His conversion
     - ☐ He feared God *(Luke 23:40)*
     - ☐ He acknowledged his sin and need for God *(Luke 23:41)*
     - ☐ He repented and believed *(Luke 23:42)*
     - ☐ He found assurance *(Luke 23:43)*
   - ☐ John 1:12
   - ☐ Acts 10:43
   - ☐ Colossians 2:6

   a. One man died **in** sin. He was a dying sinner. He died with sin in him (the cross of rejection).

   b. One man died **for** sin. He was a dying Savior. He died with sin upon Him (the cross of redemption).

   c. One man died **to** sin. He was a dying saint. He died with sin taken from him (the cross of reception).

APRIL 6

The Proof of Our Salvation in 1 John (NLT)

We can know for sure:

1. **IF WE CONFESS OUR SINS**
   - ☐ 1 John 1:9

2. **IF WE OBEY HIS COMMANDMENTS**
   - ☐ 1 John 2:3
   - ☐ 1 John 5:3

3. **IF WE DO NOT LOVE THE WORLD**
   - ☐ 1 John 2:15

4. **IF WE CONTINUE IN HIM**
   - ☐ 1 John 2:28-29

5. **IF WE DO WHAT IS RIGHT**
   - ☐ 1 John 3:10

6. **IF WE LOVE IN ACTIONS AND TRUTH**
   - ☐ 1 John 3:18
   - ☐ 1 John 4:11

7. **IF THE SPIRIT DWELLS IN US**
   - ☐ 1 John 3:24

8. **IF WE ACKNOWLEDGE JESUS CHRIST**
   - ☐ 1 John 4:15
   - ☐ 1 John 5:9

IF THESE ARE TRUE, THEN WE CAN HAVE CONFIDENCE.
- ☐ 1 John 3:21
- ☐ 1 John 4:17
- ☐ 1 John 5:14

APRIL 7

The Seven Last Words of Jesus on the Cross (NKJV)

1. "FATHER, FORGIVE THEM, THEY KNOW NOT WHAT THEY DO"
   - ☐ Luke 23:34

2. "THIS DAY YOU WILL BE WITH ME IN PARADISE"
   - ☐ Luke 23:43

3. "WOMAN, BEHOLD YOUR SON"
   - ☐ John 19:26-27

4. "MY GOD, MY GOD, WHY HAVE YOU FORSAKEN ME?"
   - ☐ Mark 15:34
   - ☐ Matthew 27:46

5. "I THIRST"
   - ☐ John 19:28

6. "IT IS FINISHED"
   - ☐ John 19:30

7. "INTO YOUR HANDS I COMMIT MY SPIRIT"
   - ☐ Luke 23:46

APRIL 8

The Seven Kinds of People God Will Not Save (NLT)

1. THE SELF-RIGHTEOUS
   - ☐ Luke 18:9-14

2. THOSE WHO REFUSE TO COME
   - ☐ John 5:39-40

3. **THE HYPOCRITE**
   - [ ] Matthew 23:13-14

4. **THOSE WHO ABANDON THE FAITH**
   - [ ] 2 Peter 2:20-22

5. **THOSE WHO HOLD TO UNBELIEF**
   - [ ] John 12:39-40

6. **THE BLASPHEMER**
   - [ ] Matthew 12:31-32

7. **ANYONE AFTER DEATH**
   - [ ] John 8:21

APRIL 9

The Seven Things God Requires of You *Deuteronomy 10:12 (NKJV)*

1. **FEAR GOD**
   - [ ] Deuteronomy 10:12

2. **WALK IN HIS WAYS**
   - [ ] Deuteronomy 10:12

3. **LOVE GOD**
   - [ ] Deuteronomy 10:12

4. **SERVE GOD**
   - [ ] Deuteronomy 10:12
   - [ ] Micah 6:8

5. **DO JUSTLY**
   - [ ] Deuteronomy 10:12

6. **LOVE MERCY**
   - [ ] Deuteronomy 10:12

7. **WALK HUMBLY WITH GOD**
   - [ ] Deuteronomy 10:12

APRIL 10

Signs of the Second Coming
Matthew 24:3 (NKJV)

1. **A GENERATION THAT REJECTS JESUS**
   - ☐ Luke 17:25-30

2. **THE RISE OF FALSE PROPHETS AND DECEPTION**
   - ☐ Matthew 24:5,11,24
   - ☐ 2 Thessalonians 2:9-11

3. **WARS AND RUMORS OF WARS**
   - ☐ Matthew 24:6
   - ☐ 1 Thessalonians 5:3

4. **INCREASE IN NATURAL DISASTERS**
   - ☐ Matthew 24:7

5. **INCREASE IN PERSECUTION TOWARD CHRISTIANS**
   - ☐ Matthew 24:9
   - ☐ Matthew 10:16-23

6. **MANY OFFENDED AND FALL AWAY**
   - ☐ Matthew 24:10
   - ☐ 1 Timothy 4:1

7. **LOVE OF MANY WILL GROW COLD**
   - ☐ Matthew 24:12

8. **GOSPEL REACHES THE END OF THE EARTH**
   - ☐ Matthew 24:14

9. **EXTREME SELFISHNESS AND MATERIALISM**
   - ☐ 2 Timothy 3:1-2

10. **SIN WILL ABOUND ON EVERY HAND**
    - ☐ 2 Timothy 3:3-5
    - ☐ Matthew 24:12

NOTES

11. **INFORMATION EXPLOSION**
    - [ ] Daniel 12:4

12. **U(NIV)ERSAL NUMBERING SYSTEM**
    - [ ] Revelation 13:16-18

Therefore, you be ready.
Matthew 24:44

APRIL 11

Seven Things God Does Not Want You to Forget (NIV)

1. **THE THINGS YOUR EYES HAVE SEEN**
   - [ ] Deuteronomy 4:9

2. **THE COVENANT YOU MADE WITH THE LORD**
   - [ ] Deuteronomy 4:23
   - [ ] 2 Kings 17:38

3. **THE LORD YOUR GOD**
   - [ ] Deuteronomy 6:12
   - [ ] Deuteronomy 8:11

4. **THE BENEFITS OF THE LORD**
   - [ ] Psalm 103:2
   - [ ] Psalm 116:12

5. **THE PRECEPTS OF THE LORD**
   - [ ] Psalm 119:61,83,109,141

6. **TO ENTERTAIN STRANGERS**
   - [ ] Hebrews 13:2

7. **TO DO GOOD AND SHARE WITH OTHERS**
   - [ ] Hebrews 13:16

NOTES

APRIL 12
The Four Blessings of Going
Genesis 12:1-2 (NKJV)

1. **GOD BLESSES THOSE WHO GO**
   - ☐ Genesis 12:1-2

2. **GOD MAKES THOSE WHO GO A BLESSING TO OTHERS**
   - ☐ Genesis 12:1-2

3. **GOD BLESSES THOSE WHO BLESS THOSE WHO GO**
   - ☐ Genesis 12:2-3

4. **GOD BLESSES ALL THOSE WHERE THEY GO** (all the families of the earth shall be blessed)
   - ☐ Genesis 12:1-2

APRIL 13
Four Ways to Overcome (NKJV)

1. **THROUGH HE WHO IS IN US**
   - ☐ 1 John 4:4
   - ☐ John 16:33
   - ☐ Romans 8:37
   - ☐ 1 Corinthians 15:57

2. **OUR FAITH**
   - ☐ 1 John 5:4-5

3. **OUR TESTIMONY**
   - ☐ Revelation 12:11

4. **BY DOING GOOD TO OTHERS**
   - ☐ Romans 12:21

APRIL 14

Four Things That Helped Jesus Through His Time of Temptation

Luke 4:1-13 (NKJV)

1. **HE WAS FULL OF THE HOLY SPIRIT**
   ☐ Luke 4:1

2. **HE WAS FASTING AND PRAYING**
   ☐ Luke 4:2

3. **HE WAS FOCUSED ON SCRIPTURE**
   ☐ Luke 4:4,8,12

4. **HE KEPT FIGHTING THE GOOD FIGHT OF FAITH UNTIL THE DEVIL FINISHED HIS ATTACK**
   ☐ Luke 4:13
   ☐ 1 Timothy 1:18
   ☐ 1 Timothy 6:12
   ☐ 2 Timothy 4:7
   ☐ Jude 1:3

APRIL 15

God is Attentive to These Prayers

2 Chronicles 6:40 (NIV)

1. **HUMILITY**
   ☐ 2 Chronicles 7:14-15

2. **FORGIVENESS**
   ☐ Nehemiah 1:5-10

3. **PRAISE**
   ☐ Nehemiah 1:11

4. RIGHTEOUSNESS
- ☐ Psalm 34:15
- ☐ 1 Peter 3:12

5. MERCY
- ☐ Psalm 130:2-4

APRIL 16
The Greatest Question of All: "What Shall We Do?" (NKJV)

- ☐ Luke 3:10-11
- ☐ Luke 3:12
- ☐ Luke 3:14
- ☐ Acts 2:37-38
- ☐ Mark 10:17

Notice the answers are all:
1. Different
2. Definite (specific)
3. Doable

APRIL 17
One Thing (NKJV)

1. I DESIRE
- ☐ Psalm 27:4

2. I DO
- ☐ Philippians 3:13

3. I KNOW
- ☐ John 9:25

4. THOU LACK
- ☐ Luke 18:22
- ☐ Mark 10:21

NOTES

5. **IS NEEDED**
   - [ ] Luke 10:42

6. **TO REMEMBER**
   - [ ] 2 Peter 3:8

7. **HAPPENS TO ALL**
   - [ ] Ecclesiastes 3:19

APRIL 18
Four Things to Do Continually
Psalm 71 (NKJV)

1. **RESORT**
   - [ ] Psalm 71:3

2. **PRAISE**
   - [ ] Psalm 71:6

3. **HOPE**
   - [ ] Psalm 71:14

4. **PROCLAIM**
   - [ ] Psalm 71:17-24

APRIL 19
Five Benefits of the Blood of Christ
Revelation 1:4-5 (NKJV)

1. **FORGIVENESS**
   - [ ] Hebrews 9:22
   - [ ] Hebrews 10:4
   - [ ] Matthew 26:28
   - [ ] Ephesians 1:7
   - [ ] Colossians 1:13-14
   - [ ] John 1:29

2. CLEANSING
- [ ] Hebrews 9:11-14
- [ ] 1 John 1:7-9
- [ ] Psalm 51:7
- [ ] Isaiah 1:18
- [ ] 1 Peter 1:2
- [ ] Hebrews 13:12

3. CONFIDENCE
- [ ] Hebrews 10:19-20
- [ ] Romans 5:9

4. NEARNESS
- [ ] Ephesians 2:13
- [ ] 1 Peter 1:18-19
- [ ] Colossians 1:20-23

5. VICTORY
- [ ] Revelation 12:11
- [ ] 1 Corinthians 15:57

BEFORE YOU PUT THE SHOVEL DOWN
- [ ] Luke 22:20

APRIL 20

God Positions Himself *Psalm 139:5 (NLT)*

1. BEFORE YOU
- [ ] Isaiah 52:12
- [ ] Deuteronomy 1:30
- [ ] Deuteronomy 9:3
- [ ] Deuteronomy 31:8
- [ ] Exodus 34:11

2. BESIDE YOU
- [ ] Psalm 16:8
- [ ] Psalm 121:5
- [ ] 2 Timothy 4:17

3. BEHIND YOU
- [ ] Isaiah 30:21
- [ ] Psalm 34:7

APRIL 21
The Six Great Commission Passages (NLT)

- ☐ Matthew 28:19-20
- ☐ Mark 16:15-18
- ☐ Luke 24:46-49
- ☐ John 20:21-23
- ☐ Acts 1:8
- ☐ Romans 1:5

APRIL 22
A Christian Should (NKJV)

1. **BE FILLED WITH THE SPIRIT**
   - ☐ Ephesians 5:18

2. **PRAY IN THE SPIRIT**
   - ☐ Jude 20
   - ☐ Ephesians 6:18

3. **SING IN THE SPIRIT**
   - ☐ Ephesians 5:19

4. **WORSHIP IN THE SPIRIT**
   - ☐ John 4:23
   - ☐ Philippians 3:3

5. **WALK IN THE SPIRIT**
   - ☐ Galatians 5:16

6. **REMEMBER THEIR BODY IS THE TEMPLE OF THE HOLY SPIRIT**
   - ☐ 1 Corinthians 6:19

APRIL 23

The Importance of Faith Mark 11:22 (NKJV)

By faith:

1. **WE LIVE**
   ☐ Romans 1:17

2. **WE STAND**
   ☐ 2 Corinthians 1:24

3. **WE WALK**
   ☐ 2 Corinthians 5:7

4. **WE FIGHT**
   ☐ 1 Timothy 6:12

5. **WE OVERCOME**
   ☐ 1 John 5:4

6. **WE ARE JUSTIFIED**
   ☐ Romans 3:25-26

7. **WE HAVE ACCESS TO GOD'S GRACE**
   ☐ Romans 5:2

APRIL 24

But Let (NKJV)

1. **PATIENCE HAVE ITS PERFECT WORK**
   ☐ James 1:4

2. **PEACE OF GOD RULE**
   ☐ Colossians 3:15

3. **WORD OF CHRIST DWELL IN YOU**
   ☐ Colossians 3:16

4. **THIS MIND BE IN YOU**
   ☐ Philippians 2:5

5. **YOUR SPEECH BE SEASONED WITH**
   - ☐ Colossians 4:6

6. **BROTHERLY LOVE CONTINUE**
   - ☐ Hebrews 13:1

7. **YOUR LIGHT SHINE**
   - ☐ Matthew 5:16

APRIL 25
The Three Back Conditions in Scripture (NKJV)

1. **BACK BITING**
   - ☐ Romans 1:30
   - ☐ Psalm 15:3
   - ☐ 2 Corinthians 12:20

2. **BACK SLIDING**
   - ☐ Hosea 11:7
   - ☐ Jeremiah 3:6-15

3. **BACKWARD LIVING**
   - ☐ Jeremiah 7:24
   - ☐ Jeremiah 15:6

APRIL 26
The Blessed Hope *Titus 2:13-14 (NKJV)*

1. **GOOD HOPE**
   - ☐ 2 Thessalonians 2:16

2. **SURE HOPE**
   - ☐ Hebrews 6:18

3. **LIVING HOPE**
   - ☐ 1 Peter 1:3

4. **PURIFYING HOPE**
   ☐ 1 John 3:3

5. **COMFORTING HOPE**
   ☐ 1 Thessalonians 4:17-18

APRIL 27
The Four "Alls" of Blessing
Psalm 100:4 AMP

1. **BLESS THE LORD ALL YOU SERVANTS**
   ☐ Psalm 134:1

2. **BLESS THE LORD AT ALL TIMES**
   ☐ Psalm 34:1
   ☐ Hebrews 13:15

3. **BLESS THE LORD WITH ALL THAT IS WITHIN ME**
   ☐ Psalm 103:1

4. **BLESS THE LORD FOR ALL HIS WORKS**
   ☐ Psalm 103:20-22

APRIL 28
The Three Times Jesus Wept (NKJV)

1. **AT LAZARUS' TOMB** (people)
   ☐ John 11:1-44

2. **AFTER THE TRIUMPHANT ENTRY**
   (He wept over the city of Jerusalem)
   ☐ Luke 19:41

3. **AT THE GARDEN** (reference to sin)
   ☐ Hebrews 5:7-9

APRIL 29

Four-part Harmony *Psalm 133:1-3 (NLT)*

- ☐ Romans 12:16
- ☐ Romans 14:19
- ☐ Romans 15:5

1. ACCEPT ONE ANOTHER
- ☐ Romans 15:7

2. FORGIVE ONE ANOTHER
- ☐ Ephesians 4:32
- ☐ Colossians 3:13
- ☐ Matthew 6:12-15

3. BE MERCIFUL TO ONE ANOTHER
- ☐ Matthew 18:33
- ☐ Matthew 5:7

4. LOVE ONE ANOTHER
- ☐ John 13:34-35
- ☐ John 15:9-17

APRIL 30

Paul's Five Great Fears (NLT)

- ☐ 2 Corinthians 12:20 (ESV)
- ☐ 2 Corinthians 12:21 (ESV)
- ☐ Galatians 4:11
- ☐ 2 Corinthians 11:3
- ☐ 1 Corinthians 9:27

MAY

MAY 1

Two Helps Toward Holiness
Acts 15:28-29 (NIV)

1. **ABSTAIN**
   - ☐ 1 Peter 2:11

2. **AVOID**
   - ☐ 1 Thessalonians 4:3
   - ☐ 1 Thessalonians 5:20-25
   - ☐ 2 Timothy 2:16
   - ☐ Titus 3:9

MAY 2

The Measure You Use Will Be Measured to You (NKJV)

In these three key areas:

1. **JUDGMENT**
   - ☐ Matthew 7:2

2. **GIVING**
   - ☐ Luke 6:38

3. **HEARING**
   - ☐ Mark 4:24

MAY 3

Definitions of Sin (NKJV)

1. **VAIN TALK**
   - ☐ Proverbs 10:19

2. **DESPISING A NEIGHBOR**
   - ☐ Proverbs 14:21

3. **FOOLISH THINKING**
   - ☐ Proverbs 24:9

4. **UNBELIEF**
   - ☐ Romans 14:20-23

5. **SHOWING PARTIALITY**
   - ☐ James 2:9

6. **KNOWING GOOD AND NOT DOING IT**
   - ☐ James 4:17

7. **LAWLESSNESS**
   - ☐ 1 John 3:4

8. **ALL UNRIGHTEOUSNESS**
   - ☐ 1 John 5:17

MAY 4

10 Things That Glorify God: [Part 1]
Ephesians 3:21 (NKJV)

1. **BEARING FRUIT**
   - ☐ John 15:8

2. **LETTING YOUR LIGHT SHINE**
   - ☐ Matthew 5:16

3. **SPIRITUAL UNITY**
   - ☐ Romans 15:6

4. **PURITY AND HOLINESS**
   - ☐ 1 Corinthians 6:18-20

5. **OBEDIENCE TO HIS CALLING**
   - ☐ 2 Thessalonians 1:11-12

MAY 5

10 Things That Glorify God: [Part 2] (NKJV)

1. **OFFERING OF EXCELLENCE**
   - ☐ 1 Corinthians 10:31

2. **PRAISE**
   - ☐ Psalm 50:23
   - ☐ Ephesians 1:6-14

3. **SUFFERING FOR CHRIST**
   - ☐ 1 Peter 4:12-16

4. **CONFESSING CHRIST**
   - ☐ Philippians 2:9-11

5. **FAITH IN STEPPING OUT**
   - ☐ Romans 4:18-20

MAY 6

Old Testament Beatitudes: [Part 1] (NKJV)

1. **BLESSED IS THE MAN WHO WALKS NOT IN THE COUNSEL OF THE UNGODLY**
   - ☐ Psalm 1:1

2. **BLESSED ARE THOSE WHO PUT THEIR TRUST IN HIM**
   - ☐ Psalm 2:12
   - ☐ Psalm 34:8
   - ☐ Psalm 40:4
   - ☐ Psalm 84:12

3. **BLESSED IS HE WHOSE SINS ARE FORGIVEN**
   - ☐ Psalm 32:1-2

4. **BLESSED IS THE NATION WHOSE GOD IS THE LORD**
   ☐ Psalm 33:12

5. **BLESSED IS HE WHO CONSIDERS THE POOR**
   ☐ Psalm 41:1

MAY 7

Old Testament Beatitudes: [Part 2] (NKJV)

1. **BLESSED IS THE MAN YOU CHOOSE**
   ☐ Psalm 65:4

2. **BLESSED ARE THOSE WHO DWELL IN YOUR HOUSE**
   ☐ Psalm 84:4

3. **BLESSED IS THE MAN WHOSE STRENGTH IS IN YOU**
   ☐ Psalm 85:5

4. **BLESSED ARE THOSE WHO KNOW THE JOYFUL SOUND**
   ☐ Psalm 89:9

5. **BLESSED IS THE MAN YOU INSTRUCT**
   ☐ Psalm 94:12

NOTES

MAY 8

The Truth About Lying: [Part 1] (NKJV)

1. **IT IS FORBIDDEN IN SCRIPTURE**
   - ☐ Exodus 20:16
   - ☐ Leviticus 19:11
   - ☐ Colossians 3:9
   - ☐ Matthew 19:18
   - ☐ 1 Peter 3:10

2. **IT IS AN ABOMINATION TO GOD**
   - ☐ Proverbs 6:16-19
   - ☐ Proverbs 12:22
   - ☐ Psalm 119:163

3. **IT IS A HINDRANCE TO YOUR RELATIONSHIP WITH GOD**
   - ☐ Isaiah 59:2-3

4. **IT IS A PRODUCT OF SATAN'S INFLUENCE IN YOUR LIFE**
   - ☐ 1 Kings 22:10-28
   - ☐ John 8:44
   - ☐ Acts 5:1-11

5. **IT BECOMES A HABIT**
   - ☐ Matthew 15:16-19

6. **IT COMES FROM THE HEART**
   - ☐ Matthew 15:18-20

MAY 9

The Truth About Lying: [Part 2] (NKJV)

1. **IT ONLY MAKES MATTERS WORSE**
   - ☐ Genesis 12:10-20

2. **IT WILL BE COMMONPLACE IN THE LAST DAYS**
   - ☐ 2 Thessalonians 2:9
   - ☐ 1 Timothy 4:2

3. **IT IS NOT FITTING FOR BELIEVERS**
   - ☐ Proverbs 13:5
   - ☐ Zephaniah 3:13
   - ☐ Proverbs 14:5
   - ☐ Ephesians 4:25

4. **IT WILL BE EXPOSED**
   - ☐ Proverbs 12:19

5. **IT CAN BE HANDLED BY CALLING ON GOD**
   - ☐ Psalm 119:29
   - ☐ Proverbs 30:8

6. **IT WILL BE PUNISHED IF NOT CONFESSED**
   - ☐ Revelation 21:8, 27
   - ☐ Revelation 22:15
   - ☐ Psalm 101:7
   - ☐ Psalm 5:6
   - ☐ Proverbs 19:5,9

MAY 10

Bad Things You Can Be Filled With
Romans 1:29, Galatians 5:19 (NKJV)

1. **ENVY**
   - ☐ Acts 13:45

2. **WRATH**
   - ☐ Luke 4:28

3. **RAGE**
   - ☐ Luke 6:11

4. **SORROW**
   - ☐ John 16:6

5. **LIES**
   - ☐ Acts 5:3

6. **ANGER**
   - ☐ Acts 5:17

MAY 11

Six Things the Bible Teaches Us About Light (NKJV)

1. **WE ARE CALLED OUT OF DARKNESS INTO THE LIGHT**
   - ☐ Romans 13:12
   - ☐ Isaiah 9:2
   - ☐ Matthew 6:23
   - ☐ Acts 26:17-18
   - ☐ Matthew 4:16

2. **WE ARE TO STEP INTO THE LIGHT**
   - ☐ John 3:16-21

NOTES

3. WE ARE TO WALK IN THE LIGHT
- ☐ 1 John 1:7
- ☐ Ephesians 5:8
- ☐ John 11:10

4. WE ARE TO BEAR WITNESS OF THE LIGHT
- ☐ John 1:7-8
- ☐ John 8:12
- ☐ John 9:5

5. WE ARE TO LET OUR LIGHT SHINE
- ☐ Matthew 5:14-16
- ☐ John 5:35
- ☐ Philippians 2:15

6. WE ARE TO BE FULL OF LIGHT
- ☐ Luke 11:34-36

MAY 12

Five Truths About Darkness (NKJV)

1. THE LIGHT SHINES IN THE DARKNESS AND THE DARKNESS CANNOT OVERCOME IT
- ☐ John 1:5

2. WE ARE TO HAVE NO FELLOWSHIP WITH DARKNESS
- ☐ 2 Corinthians 6:14

3. WE ARE TO EXPOSE THE WORKS OF DARKNESS
- ☐ Ephesians 5:11

4. WE ARE TO BE DELIVERED FROM THE STRONGHOLD OF DARKNESS
- ☐ Colossians 1:13

5. WE ARE TO REMOVE THE WORKS OF DARKNESS
- ☐ Romans 13:12

NOTES

MAY 13

Five Things We Are Commanded to Put On (NKJV)

1. **THE ARMOR OF LIGHT**
   - ☐ Romans 13:12

2. **THE LORD JESUS CHRIST**
   - ☐ Romans 13:14
   - ☐ Galatians 3:27

3. **THE NEW MAN**
   - ☐ Ephesians 4:24
   - ☐ Colossians 3:10

4. **THE WHOLE ARMOR OF GOD**
   - ☐ Ephesians 6:11

5. **THE FRUIT OF THE SPIRIT**
   - ☐ Colossians 3:12-14
   - ☐ Galatians 5:22

MAY 14

Six "Be" Commands in Ephesians (NKJV)

1. **BE RENEWED**
   - ☐ Ephesians 4:23

2. **BE ANGRY AND SIN NOT**
   - ☐ Ephesians 4:26

3. **BE KIND TO ONE ANOTHER**
   - ☐ Ephesians 4:32

4. **BE FOLLOWERS OF GOD**
   - ☐ Ephesians 5:1

5. **BE FILLED WITH THE SPIRIT**
   ☐ Ephesians 5:18

6. **BE STRONG IN THE LORD**
   ☐ Ephesians 6:10

MAY 15
The Seven Gifts of Christ (NKJV)

1. **REST**
   ☐ Matthew 11:28

2. **KEYS OF THE KINGDOM**
   ☐ Matthew 16:19

3. **POWER OVER EVIL SPIRITS**
   ☐ Luke 10:19

4. **LIVING WATER**
   ☐ John 4:14

5. **ETERNAL LIFE**
   ☐ John 10:28

6. **MY PEACE**
   ☐ John 14:27

7. **MEASURE OF FAITH**
   ☐ Romans 12:3

MAY 16
Seven Observations About Thorns in the Bible *Acts 7:30-35 NASB*

1. **THEY ARE THE RESULT OF LIVING IN A FALLEN WORLD**
   ☐ Genesis 3:17-18

2. **THEY MULTIPLY THROUGH DISOBEDIENCE**
   - ☐ Numbers 33:55
   - ☐ Joshua 23:12-13

3. **THEY CAN CHOKE THE LIFE OUT OF US**
   - ☐ Matthew 13:1-23

4. **SATAN USES THORNS TO TROUBLE AND TORMENT US**
   - ☐ 2 Corinthians 12:7

5. **PRAYER DOES NOT ALWAYS REMOVE THEM**
   - ☐ 2 Corinthians 12:8

6. **THEY ARE A REMINDER THAT GOD'S GRACE IS SUFFICIENT**
   - ☐ 2 Corinthians 12:9-10

7. **JESUS WORE A CROWN OF THEM FOR US**
   - ☐ Matthew 27:29
   - ☐ John 19:2-5

BEFORE YOU PUT THE SHOVEL DOWN
   - ☐ Isaiah 55:6-13 (NLT)

MAY 17

Six Things God Desires More Than Sacrifice *Mark 12:28-34 (NIV)*

1. **A LIFE OF OBEDIENCE**
   - ☐ 1 Samuel 15:22
   - ☐ Jeremiah 7:21-23

2. **A COMMITMENT TO DO WHAT IS RIGHT**
   - ☐ Proverbs 21:3

3. **A LOYAL RELATIONSHIP WITH HIM**
   - ☐ Hosea 6:6

4. AN ATTITUDE OF MERCY
- ☐ Matthew 12:7
- ☐ Matthew 9:13

5. A DESIRE TO DRAW NEAR
- ☐ Ecclesiastes 5:1 (ESV)

6. A BROKEN AND CONTRITE HEART
- ☐ Psalm 51:16-17
- ☐ Psalm 40:6-8
- ☐ Isaiah 1:11

MAY 18

Six Spiritual Priorities You Can't Afford to Neglect (NKJV)

1. THE GIFT OF SALVATION
- ☐ Hebrews 2:3
- ☐ Philippians 2:12-13

2. THE WORD OF GOD AND PRAYER
- ☐ Acts 6:2-4 (NLT)
- ☐ Psalm 119:16 (NIV)

3. THE NEEDS OF OTHERS
- ☐ Acts 6:1
- ☐ Hebrews 13:2 (AMP)
- ☐ Hebrews 13:16 (AMP)

4. THE SPIRITUAL GIFT GOD HAS GIVEN YOU
- ☐ 1 Timothy 4:14 (AMP)
- ☐ 2 Timothy 1:6

5. THE WILL AND WISDOM OF GOD IN YOUR LIFE
- ☐ Joshua 18:3
- ☐ Proverbs 8:33 (ESV)

6. THE IMPORTANCE OF MEETING TOGETHER (for worship)
- ☐ Hebrews 10:25 (NLT)

NOTES

MAY 19

Divine Discipline (NLT)

Two kinds of discipline:

1. **SELF-DISCIPLINE**
   ☐ 2 Timothy 1:7

2. **DIVINE DISCIPLINE**
   ☐ Hebrews 12:5-12

Three reminders about divine discipline:

1. **DO NOT DESPISE DISCIPLINE**
   ☐ Hebrews 12:5

2. **DO NOT BE DISCOURAGED BY DISCIPLINE**
   ☐ Hebrews 12:5

3. **DO NOT DISCONTINUE UNDER THE LORD'S DISCIPLINE**
   ☐ Hebrews 12:7

Divine discipline means:

1. **YOU ARE LOVED**
   ☐ Hebrews 12:6
   ☐ Proverbs 3:11-12
   ☐ Revelation 3:19

2. **YOU ARE A LEGITIMATE CHILD OF GOD**
   ☐ Hebrews 12:6-8

3. **YOU ARE RECEIVING THIS FOR YOUR OWN GOOD**
   ☐ Hebrews 12:10
   ☐ Deuteronomy 8:5
   ☐ Isaiah 38:16

4. **YOU ARE BEING MADE INTO HIS LIKENESS**
   ☐ Hebrews 12:10

5. **YOU ARE FACING A HARVEST AHEAD**
   ☐ Hebrews 12:11

6. **YOU WILL EXPERIENCE PEACE AFTER GOING THROUGH THE PAIN**
   ☐ Hebrews 12:11

MAY 20
You're Only Fooling Yourself When (NLT)

1. **YOU THINK YOU ARE TOO IMPORTANT TO HELP OTHERS**
   ☐ Galatians 6:3

2. **YOU LISTEN TO THE WORD BUT DON'T LIVE IT**
   ☐ James 1:22
   ☐ Psalm 119:118

3. **YOU CLAIM TO BE RELIGIOUS BUT DON'T CONTROL YOUR TONGUE**
   ☐ James 1:26

4. **YOU CLAIM TO BE WITHOUT SIN**
   ☐ 1 John 1:8

BEFORE YOU PUT THE SHOVEL DOWN
   ☐ 1 Corinthians 3:18 (TLB)

MAY 21

Is Anything Too Hard for the Lord?
Numbers 11:23 (NKJV)

- [ ] Genesis 18:14
- [ ] Jeremiah 32:17,27
- [ ] Luke 1:37
- [ ] Matthew 19:26
- [ ] Mark 9:23
- [ ] Mark 10:27
- [ ] Luke 18:27
- [ ] Philippians 4:13
- [ ] Romans 4:21
- [ ] 1 Samuel 14:6
- [ ] Job 42:2

MAY 22

The Answers for Unanswered Prayer (NKJV)

Some context:

- [ ] Habakkuk 1:2
- [ ] Lamentations 3:8
- [ ] Psalm 13:1-2
- [ ] Jeremiah 11:11
- [ ] Zechariah 7:13

What things can hinder our prayers?

1. UNCONFESSED SIN
- [ ] Isaiah 59:2
- [ ] Psalm 66:18
- [ ] Micah 3:4

2. IGNORING GOD'S LAW
- [ ] Proverbs 1:24-28; 28:9

3. **SHUTTING OUR EARS TO THE CRY OF THE POOR**
   ☐ Proverbs 21:13

4. **WRONG MOTIVES**
   ☐ James 4:2-3

5. **LACK OF FAITH**
   ☐ James 1:5-8

6. **PRAYING OUTSIDE OF GOD'S WILL**
   ☐ 1 John 5:14-15

7. **PRIDE**
   ☐ Luke 18:10-14
   ☐ 2 Chronicles 7:14

8. **UNFORGIVENESS**
   ☐ Mark 11:25-26

9. **HYPOCRISY**
   ☐ Matthew 6:5
   ☐ Mark 12:40

10. **DISHONORABLE BEHAVIOR**
    ☐ Proverbs 15:8

11. **FAILURE TO ASK**
    ☐ James 4:2

12. **LACK OF PERSISTENCE IN PRAYER**
    ☐ Luke 18:1-8

13. **IDOLATRY OR MISPLACED PRIORITIES**
    ☐ Ezekiel 14:3
    ☐ James 4:3-5

14. **UNHEALTHY RELATIONSHIP WITH SPOUSE**
    ☐ 1 Peter 3:7

NOTES

MAY 23

The God Who Sees *Genesis 16:13 (NLT)*

- ☐ Genesis 29:31
- ☐ Genesis 31:42
- ☐ Exodus 2:23-25
- ☐ Exodus 3:7
- ☐ 2 Chronicles 16:9
- ☐ Nehemiah 9:9
- ☐ Psalm 33:13
- ☐ Proverbs 5:21
- ☐ Proverbs 15:3
- ☐ Jonah 3:10
- ☐ Luke 7:13

MAY 24

What Does It Profit? (NKJV)

1. **WHAT IS THE PROFIT OF ALL THE WORK?**
   - ☐ Ecclesiastes 1:3; 3:9; 5:11,16

2. **WHAT DOES IT PROFIT IF YOU GAIN THE WHOLE WORLD AND LOSE YOUR OWN SOUL?**
   - ☐ Matthew 16:26
   - ☐ Mark 8:36

3. **WHAT DOES IT PROFIT IF YOU HAVE FAITH AND NOT WORKS?**
   - ☐ James 2:14-16

NOTES

MAY 25
Life in Christ (NKJV)

What does life in Christ look like?

1. **NEWNESS OF LIFE**
   - [ ] Romans 6:4

2. **LIGHT OF LIFE**
   - [ ] John 8:12

3. **ABUNDANT LIFE**
   - [ ] John 10:10

4. **ETERNAL LIFE**
   - [ ] John 17:3

5. **CROWN OF LIFE**
   - [ ] James 1:12

MAY 26
A Simple Prayer *Psalm 30:10 (NLT)*

1. **HEAR ME**
   - [ ] Psalm 30:10

2. **HAVE MERCY ON ME**
   - [ ] Psalm 30:10

3. **HELP ME**
   - [ ] Psalm 30:10

NOTES

MAY 27
Two Kinds of Appearance to Avoid (KJV/ESV)

1. **THE APPEARANCE OF EVIL**
   - ☐ 1 Thessalonians 5:22-24 (KJV)

2. **THE APPEARANCE OF GODLINESS**
   - ☐ 2 Timothy 3:1-9 (ESV)

BEFORE YOU PUT THE SHOVEL DOWN
- ☐ 1 Samuel 16:7

MAY 28
Six Reasons Not to Judge (NLT)

1. **YOU DON'T HAVE A RIGHT, THERE IS ONLY ONE JUDGE**
   - ☐ James 4:11-12
   - ☐ Romans 14:4

2. **BECAUSE JESUS SAID SO**
   - ☐ Matthew 7:1

3. **BECAUSE THE MEASURE YOU USE WILL BE MEASURED BACK TO YOU**
   - ☐ Matthew 7:2

4. **BECAUSE IT EXPOSES YOUR EVIL THOUGHTS**
   - ☐ James 2:2-4

5. **BECAUSE NOW IS NOT THE TIME TO JUDGE**
   - ☐ 1 Corinthians 4:5

6. **BECAUSE YOU WILL NOT ESCAPE GOD'S JUDGMENT IF YOU DO**
   - ☐ Romans 2:1-3

BEFORE YOU PUT THE SHOVEL DOWN
- ☐ Romans 14:3-13

MAY 29

To Enjoy Life and See Many Happy Days 1 Peter 3:10-12 (NKJV)

1. **REFRAIN YOUR TONGUE FROM EVIL**
   ☐ 1 Peter 3:10

2. **KEEP YOUR LIPS FROM SPEAKING LIES**
   ☐ 1 Peter 3:10b

3. **TURN AWAY FROM EVIL**
   ☐ 1 Peter 3:11

4. **DO GOOD**
   ☐ 1 Peter 3:11b

5. **PURSUE PEACE**
   ☐ 1 Peter 3:11c

MAY 30

The Carnality of Partiality (NKJV)

1. **IT IS NOT GOOD**
   ☐ Proverbs 24:23
   ☐ Proverbs 28:21

2. **IT IS CONTRARY TO THE CHARACTER OF GOD**
   ☐ Deuteronomy 10:17
   ☐ Romans 2:11
   ☐ Ephesians 6:9
   ☐ Acts 10:34
   ☐ Matthew 22:16

3. **IT IS INCONSISTENT WITH OUR FAITH CLAIMS**
   ☐ James 2:1

4. **IT IS INCOMPATIBLE WITH "THINGS ABOVE"**
   ☐ James 3:17

5. **IT IS SIN**
   ☐ James 2:9

6. **IT PUTS YOU IN A POSITION OF JUDGMENT**
   ☐ Matthew 7:1

BEFORE YOU PUT THE SHOVEL DOWN
   ☐ 1 Timothy 5:21

MAY 31
Three Dangers in Our Spiritual Journey (NKJV)

1. **STRAYING**
   ☐ Isaiah 53:6
   ☐ Psalm 95:10
   ☐ Matthew 18:12-13
   ☐ 1 Peter 2:25

2. **WANDERING**
   ☐ James 5:19
   ☐ Psalm 119:10
   ☐ Proverbs 21:16
   ☐ Jeremiah 14:10

3. **DRIFTING**
   ☐ Hebrews 2:1

JUNE

JUNE 1

God is the Author Of (NKJV)

1. **PEACE**
   - ☐ 1 Corinthians 14:33

2. **SALVATION**
   - ☐ Hebrews 5:9

3. **FAITH**
   - ☐ Hebrews 12:2

JUNE 2

Three Temperatures of the Heart (NKJV)

1. **COLD**
   - ☐ Matthew 24:12

2. **LUKEWARM**
   - ☐ Revelation 3:15-16

3. **BURNING**
   - ☐ Luke 24:32
   - ☐ Psalm 39:3

JUNE 3

You Cannot...Unless (NKJV)

1. **YOU CANNOT SEE THE KINGDOM OF GOD UNLESS YOU ARE BORN AGAIN**
   - ☐ John 3:3
   - ☐ John 3:5

2. **YOU CANNOT BE FRUITFUL UNLESS YOU REMAIN IN CHRIST**
   - ☐ John 15:4

3. **YOU CANNOT RECEIVE ANYTHING UNLESS IT COMES FROM ABOVE**
   - [ ] John 3:27

4. **YOU CANNOT WIN THE PRIZE UNLESS YOU FOLLOW THE RULES**
   - [ ] 2 Timothy 2:5
   - [ ] 1 Corinthians 9:24

JUNE 4
The Basics of Being Born Again
2 Corinthians 5:17 (NLT)

1. **YOU MUST BE BORN AGAIN**
   - [ ] John 3:7

2. **YOU CANNOT SEE THE KINGDOM UNLESS YOU ARE BORN AGAIN**
   - [ ] John 3:3

3. **YOU ARE BORN AGAIN THROUGH GOD'S MERCY**
   - [ ] 1 Peter 1:3
   - [ ] Titus 3:5

4. **YOU CANNOT BE BORN AGAIN WITHOUT THE WATER AND THE SPIRIT**
   - [ ] John 3:5-6

5. **YOU ARE BORN AGAIN NOT FOR THE SHORT-TERM BUT FOR THE LONG-TERM**
   - [ ] 1 Peter 1:23

"If you have been born only once, you will have to die twice. But if you have been born twice, you will have to die only once (and you may even escape that one death if Jesus returns to the earth during your lifetime)."
—David Jeremiah, *What Are You Afraid Of?*

JUNE 5

Five Good Things That Will Not Get You to Heaven (NKJV)

1. **GOOD WORKS**
   - ☐ Ephesians 2:8-9
   - ☐ 2 Timothy 1:9

2. **GOOD BEHAVIOR**
   - ☐ Mark 10:18

3. **GOOD INTENTIONS**
   - ☐ Matthew 25:1-13

4. **GOOD GIFTS** (money)
   - ☐ Acts 8:18-20

5. **GOOD CONNECTIONS**
   - ☐ Ezekiel 18:20

JUNE 6

The Marks of a Great Church (NIV)

1. **GREAT BOLDNESS**
   - ☐ Acts 4:29
   - ☐ Acts 4:13 (NKJV)
   - ☐ Acts 28:31
   - ☐ 1 Timothy 3:13 (NKJV)

2. **GREAT POWER AND GREAT GRACE**
   - ☐ Acts 4:33
   - ☐ Acts 6:8

3. **GREAT FEAR**
   - ☐ Acts 5:5-11
   - ☐ Acts 9:31

4. **GREAT JOY**
   - ☐ Acts 8:8
   - ☐ Acts 2:46 (NLT)

- [ ] Acts 15:3 (NKJV)
- [ ] Acts 15:31 (NLT)

5. **GREAT EAGERNESS**
   - [ ] Acts 17:11

6. **GREAT HUMILITY**
   - [ ] Acts 20:19

7. **GREAT PERSECUTION**
   - [ ] Acts 8:1
   - [ ] Acts 9:16 (KJV)
   - [ ] Acts 19:23

Because of these great things going on…a great number of people were turning to the Lord (Acts 11:21,24,26; 14:1).

JUNE 7

The Unfavorable Nature of Favoritism *Proverbs 24:23 (NIV)*

Favoritism is unfavorable:

1. **BECAUSE GOD DOES NOT SHOW FAVORITISM**
   - [ ] Acts 10:34
   - [ ] Romans 2:11
   - [ ] Galatians 2:6
   - [ ] Ephesians 6:9

2. **BECAUSE FAVORITISM IS SIN**
   - [ ] James 2:9

3. **BECAUSE WE ARE COMMANDED NOT TO SHOW FAVORITISM**
   - [ ] James 2:1
   - [ ] Exodus 23:3
   - [ ] Leviticus 19:15
   - [ ] Malachi 2:9
   - [ ] 1 Timothy 5:21

NOTES

4. **BECAUSE CHRIST DID NOT SHOW FAVORITISM**
   ☐ Luke 20:21

5. **BECAUSE FAVORITISM IS NOT WISE**
   ☐ James 3:17

JUNE 8
The Six Sins of Sodom and Gomorrah
Genesis 19:1-29 (NKJV)

1. **PRIDE**
   ☐ Ezekiel 16:49

2. **FULLNESS OF FOOD**
   ☐ Ezekiel 16:49b

3. **ABUNDANCE OF IDLENESS**
   ☐ Ezekiel 16:49c

4. **IGNORING THE POOR AND NEEDY**
   ☐ Ezekiel 16:49d

5. **HAUGHTY IN SPIRIT**
   ☐ Ezekiel 16:50

6. **COMMITTED ABOMINATIONS BEFORE GOD**
   ☐ Ezekiel 16:50b

BEFORE YOU PUT THE SHOVEL DOWN
   ☐ Isaiah 1:9
   ☐ Romans 9:29

JUNE 9
The Benefits to Those Who Fear God (NLT)

1. **THE LORD IS A FRIEND**
   ☐ Psalm 25:14

2. **HIS SALVATION IS NEAR**
   ☐ Psalm 85:9

3. **HE GIVES HIS UNFAILING LOVE**
   ☐ Psalm 103:11,17

4. **HE IS COMPASSIONATE**
   ☐ Psalm 103:13

5. **HE SUPPLIES THEIR NEEDS**
   ☐ Psalm 111:5

6. **THEIR NAMES ARE REMEMBERED AND RECORDED**
   ☐ Malachi 3:16

JUNE 10
The Tongue James 3:1-12 (NLT)

1. **THE TONGUE IS SMALL, BUT IT CAN CAUSE BIG PROBLEMS**
   ☐ James 3:3-5

2. **THE TONGUE IS WHAT CONTROLS THE REST OF THE BODY**
   ☐ James 3:3-4

3. **THE TONGUE IS A FIRE SET ON FIRE FROM HELL**
   ☐ James 3:6

NOTES

4. **THE TONGUE CANNOT BE TAMED ON ITS OWN**
   - ☐ James 3:9

5. **THE TONGUE SHOULD NOT BLESS AND BLAST**
   - ☐ James 3:10

JUNE 11

Regarding the Righteous [NLT]

There are those who:

1. **THINK THEY ARE RIGHTEOUS**
   - ☐ Mark 2:17

2. **APPEAR TO BE RIGHTEOUS**
   - ☐ Luke 16:15
   - ☐ Matthew 23:28

3. **RELY ON THEIR OWN RIGHTEOUSNESS**
   - ☐ Luke 18:9

4. **ARE TRULY RIGHTEOUS IN CHRIST**
   - ☐ Romans 4:5
   - ☐ 1 John 3:7
   - ☐ 2 Peter 2:7-8
   - ☐ James 2:23
   - ☐ Hebrews 11:4,7
   - ☐ Philippians 3:6-9

BEFORE YOU PUT THE SHOVEL DOWN
- ☐ 2 Timothy 2:22
- ☐ Matthew 13:43-49

JUNE 12

Seven Things the Godly Will Follow After *Matthew 10:38 KJV*

1. **PEACE**
   - ☐ Romans 14:19
   - ☐ Hebrews 12:14

2. **RIGHTEOUSNESS**
   - ☐ 1 Timothy 6:11

3. **GODLINESS**
   - ☐ 1 Timothy 6:11

4. **FAITH**
   - ☐ 1 Timothy 6:11

5. **LOVE**
   - ☐ 1 Timothy 6:11
   - ☐ 1 Corinthians 14:1

6. **PATIENCE**
   - ☐ 1 Timothy 6:11

7. **MEEKNESS**
   - ☐ 1 Timothy 6:11

JUNE 13

The Eight Things God Hates
Proverbs 6:16-19 (NLT)

1. **HAUGHTY EYES**
   - ☐ Proverbs 6:17

2. **LYING TONGUE**
   - ☐ Proverbs 6:17

3. **HANDS THAT KILL THE INNOCENT**
   - ☐ Proverbs 6:17
   - ☐ Psalm 11:5

NOTES

4. **A HEART THAT PLOTS EVIL**
   - ☐ Proverbs 6:18
   - ☐ Proverbs 8:13

5. **FEET THAT RUN TO DO WRONG**
   - ☐ Proverbs 6:18

6. **A FALSE WITNESS**
   - ☐ Proverbs 6:19

7. **A PERSON WHO SOWS DISCORD**
   - ☐ Proverbs 6:19

8. **WORSHIP OF OTHER GODS**
   - ☐ Deuteronomy 12:31
   - ☐ Deuteronomy 16:21-22

JUNE 14

What It Means to Follow Christ:

[Part 1] *Matthew 4:19 (NKJV)*

Following Christ means:

1. **I AM IN THE PROCESS OF BECOMING WHAT HE HAS CALLED ME TO BE**
   - ☐ Matthew 4:19
   - ☐ Philippians 1:6

2. **I AM PRACTICING THE DISCIPLINE OF IMMEDIATE OBEDIENCE**
   - ☐ Matthew 4:19-22
   - ☐ Matthew 9:9

3. **MY WORDS ARE MORE THAN RHETORIC AND HAVE MEANING**
   - ☐ Matthew 8:19-20
   - ☐ Matthew 15:8

4. **I HAVE SURRENDERED THE FIRST PLACE POSITION IN MY LIFE TO CHRIST**
   - ☐ Matthew 8:21-22

5. **I AM NOT ONLY EMBRACING THE CROSS BUT ENDURING IT AS WELL**
   - ☐ Matthew 10:38
   - ☐ Matthew 16:24
   - ☐ Luke 9:23

JUNE 15
What It Means to Follow Christ: [Part 2] [NKJV]

Following Christ means:

1. **I HAVE SURRENDERED EVERY AREA OF MY LIFE TO CHRIST, INCLUDING MY FINANCES**
   - ☐ Matthew 19:21
   - ☐ Mark 10:21-22

2. **I AM FOLLOWING THE EXAMPLE OF CHRIST**
   - ☐ 1 Peter 2:21
   - ☐ 1 Corinthians 11:1-2

3. **I AM ACTIVELY SERVING THE LORD**
   - ☐ John 12:26

4. **I AM WALKING IN THE LIGHT, NOT IN DARKNESS**
   - ☐ John 8:12

5. **I AM LISTENING TO THE VOICE OF THE LORD**
   - ☐ John 10:27

NOTES

6. **I AM DETERMINED I WILL NOT TURN BACK AGAIN**
   ☐ John 6:66 (NIV)
   ☐ John 8:12

7. **I AM FOLLOWING CHRIST WITHOUT DISTRACTION**
   ☐ John 21:19-22

JUNE 16

The Marks of True Greatness

Matthew 18:1-4 (NLT)

There is the way the WORLD measures greatness.

There is the way the WORD measures greatness.

And they are completely different.

According to the WORD, the greatest are those who:

1. **OBEY GOD'S LAWS**
   ☐ Matthew 5:19

2. **TEACH GOD'S LAWS**
   ☐ Matthew 5:19
   ☐ Deuteronomy 4:5-8
   ☐ Matthew 28:20

3. **ARE HUMBLE**
   ☐ Matthew 18:4

4. **SERVE**
   ☐ Matthew 20:25-28
   ☐ Matthew 23:11-12

5. **LOVE**
   ☐ 1 Corinthians 13:13

6. BELIEVE
- [ ] Genesis 12:1-2

7. ENDURED SUFFERING
- [ ] Psalm 71:20-21
- [ ] Job 1:3 (NKJV)
- [ ] Psalm 66:12

JUNE 17
Stop Signs in Scripture: [Part 1] (NLT)
- [ ] Deuteronomy 10:16
- [ ] 1 Samuel 2:3
- [ ] Psalm 75:4
- [ ] Psalm 37:8
- [ ] Proverbs 17:14
- [ ] Isaiah 1:13
- [ ] Isaiah 1:16 (NIV)
- [ ] Zechariah 1:4
- [ ] John 2:16
- [ ] John 5:14

JUNE 18
Stop Signs in Scripture: [Part 2] (NLT)
- [ ] John 6:43
- [ ] John 7:24 (NIV)
- [ ] John 20:27 (NIV)
- [ ] Romans 14:13
- [ ] 1 Corinthians 3:18
- [ ] 1 Corinthians 15:34
- [ ] Ephesians 4:25
- [ ] Zechariah 8:17
- [ ] 2 Timothy 2:14
- [ ] Hebrews 6:1
- [ ] 2 Peter 2:14 (NIV)
- [ ] Jeremiah 26:13
- [ ] Ezekiel 14:6
- [ ] Daniel 4:27

NOTES

JUNE 19
The "Above Alls" in Scripture (NLT)

- [ ] Philippians 1:27
- [ ] Matthew 6:33
- [ ] Colossians 3:14
- [ ] 1 Peter 4:8 (NIV)
- [ ] 2 Peter 1:20-21
- [ ] James 5:12 (NKJV)
- [ ] Ephesians 6:16 (NKJV)
- [ ] 2 Peter 3:3 (NIV)
- [ ] Proverbs 4:23 (NIV)

JUNE 20
Two Spiritual Threats (NIV)

1. **IMPURITY**
   - [ ] Hebrews 13:4
   - [ ] Colossians 3:5
   - [ ] Ephesians 5:3-17

2. **IMMATURITY**
   - [ ] 1 Corinthians 13:11
   - [ ] Hebrews 5:12-14
   - [ ] Hebrews 6:1

JUNE 21
Seven Marks of Spiritually Mature Christians *Philippians 3:12-31 (NLT)*

1. **THEY HAVE A DIVINE PERSPECTIVE ON THEIR ACHIEVEMENTS**
   - [ ] Philippians 3:12-13
   - [ ] 1 Timothy 4:15

2. **THEY CAREFULLY OVERSEE HOW THEY AGREE AND DISAGREE**
   - ☐ Philippians 3:15
   - ☐ Philippians 2:2

3. **THEY ARE TEACHABLE**
   - ☐ Philippians 3:15b

4. **THEY DON'T REGRESS IN THE PROGRESS THAT THEY ALREADY POSSESS**
   - ☐ Philippians 3:16
   - ☐ Luke 9:62
   - ☐ 1 Corinthians 9:24-27

5. **THEY ARE FOLLOWING THE PATTERN OF GODLY EXAMPLES**
   - ☐ Philippians 3:17
   - ☐ Philippians 4:9
   - ☐ 1 Corinthians 4:16
   - ☐ Hebrews 13:7

6. **THEY EMBRACE THE CROSS**
   - ☐ Philippians 3:18
   - ☐ Matthew 16:24-26
   - ☐ 1 Corinthians 1:18

7. **THEY SET THEIR MINDS ON THINGS ABOVE**
   - ☐ Philippians 3:19
   - ☐ Colossians 3:1-2
   - ☐ Matthew 16:23

BEFORE YOU PUT THE SHOVEL DOWN
   - ☐ Ephesians 4:13-16
   - ☐ Colossians 1:28
   - ☐ James 1:4

NOTES

JUNE 22

Paul's 10 Commandments for Living in a Crooked and Perverse Generation *Philippians 2:12-18 (NLT)*

1. **KEEP FOLLOWING BIBLICAL INSTRUCTION**
   - [ ] Philippians 2:12a,16

2. **BEAR FRUIT**
   - [ ] Philippians 2:12b

3. **OBEY GOD WITH DEEP REVERENCE AND FEAR**
   - [ ] Philippians 2:12c

4. **CONTINUE TO LET GOD COMPLETE HIS WORK**
   - [ ] Philippians 2:13a

5. **BE FULLY PLEASING TO GOD**
   - [ ] Philippians 2:13b

6. **STOP COMPLAINING**
   - [ ] Philippians 2:14

7. **FOCUS ON LIVING RIGHT INSTEAD OF WHAT EVERYONE ELSE IS DOING WRONG**
   - [ ] Philippians 2:15a

8. **LET YOUR LIGHT SHINE IN THE DARKNESS**
   - [ ] Philippians 2:15b

9. **STAY TRUE AND FAITHFUL**
   - [ ] Philippians 2:17

10. **DON'T LOSE YOUR JOY**
    - [ ] Philippians 2:18

BEFORE YOU PUT THE SHOVEL DOWN
- [ ] Acts 2:40
- [ ] 2 Peter 3:11-14

JUNE 23

The Benefits of Belonging to Christ [NKJV]

1. **NO CONDEMNATION**
   - ☐ Romans 8:1-2
   - ☐ John 3:18-19 (NIV)
   - ☐ John 13:8

2. **VICTORY OVER SIN**
   - ☐ Galatians 5:24
   - ☐ Galatians 2:20
   - ☐ 2 Timothy 2:19

3. **GUIDANCE FROM THE HOLY SPIRIT**
   - ☐ Romans 8:9

4. **GRATITUDE AND THANKFULNESS IN YOUR HEART**
   - ☐ 1 Thessalonians 5:18

5. **A CONSCIENCE THAT IS CLEAR**
   - ☐ 1 Peter 3:16

6. **PARTICIPATION IN THE BODY OF CHRIST**
   - ☐ 2 Corinthians 10:7
   - ☐ Romans 12:4-5

7. **A VOICE YOU CAN TRUST**
   - ☐ John 8:47
   - ☐ Romans 1:6
   - ☐ 1 Corinthians 15:22-23

BEFORE YOU PUT THE SHOVEL DOWN
   - ☐ Ephesians 3:6

JUNE 24

The Secret of Contentment
Philippians 4:10-13 (NIV)

1. **CONTENTMENT IS A PERSONAL PURSUIT**
   - ☐ Philippians 4:11-12
   - ☐ James 4:2

2. **CONTENTMENT IS AN ATTITUDE THAT IS LEARNED**
   - ☐ Philippians 4:11-12

3. **CONTENTMENT SHOULD BE CONSISTENT**
   - ☐ Philippians 4:11-12
   - ☐ Luke 3:14
   - ☐ 1 Timothy 6:8
   - ☐ Hebrews 13:5

4. **TRUE CONTENTMENT IS NOT BASED ON OUR CIRCUMSTANCES**
   - ☐ Philippians 4:11-12
   - ☐ 2 Corinthians 12:10

5. **CONTENTMENT IS FOUND IN A PERSON NOT IN POSSESSIONS**
   - ☐ Philippians 4:13
   - ☐ 2 Corinthians 3:5
   - ☐ 2 Corinthians 9:8
   - ☐ Hebrews 13:5

BEFORE YOU PUT THE SHOVEL DOWN
- ☐ 1 Timothy 6:6-10

JUNE 25

The Fruit of Righteousness: [Part 1]
Philippians 1:9-11 (NKJV)

Paul prays five things for the Philippian church:

1. **THAT YOUR LOVE MAY ABOUND STILL MORE AND MORE**
   - ☐ Philippians 1:9
   - ☐ John 13:35

2. **THAT YOU MAY APPROVE THE THINGS THAT ARE EXCELLENT**
   - ☐ Philippians 1:10a
   - ☐ Philippians 4:8

3. **THAT YOU MAY BE SINCERE AND WITHOUT OFFENSE UNTIL THE DAY OF CHRIST**
   - ☐ Philippians 1:10b
   - ☐ 2 Corinthians 5:10

4. **THAT YOU ARE BEING FILLED WITH THE FRUITS OF RIGHTEOUSNESS**
   - ☐ Philippians 1:11a
   - ☐ Romans 6:22
   - ☐ James 3:17-18

5. **THAT GOD MAY BE GLORIFIED AND PRAISED**
   - ☐ Philippians 1:11b
   - ☐ Matthew 5:16
   - ☐ Colossians 1:10
   - ☐ John 15:8
   - ☐ 1 Peter 4:11

BEFORE YOU PUT THE SHOVEL DOWN
The first three produce the fourth (fruit), and the fourth results in the fifth (pleasing and glorifying God).

NOTES

JUNE 26

The Fruit of Righteousness: [Part 2]

Philippians 1:9-11 (NKJV)

Five fruit facts to keep in mind:

1. **BEARING FRUIT IS EXPECTED IN THE CHRISTIAN LIFE**
   - ☐ Matthew 3:8
   - ☐ Luke 3:8
   - ☐ John 15:16
   - ☐ 2 Peter 1:8

2. **BEARING FRUIT WILL BE INSPECTED**
   - ☐ Matthew 3:10
   - ☐ John 15:2,6
   - ☐ Matthew 7:16-20
   - ☐ Mark 11:12-25

3. **BEARING FRUIT CAN BE INFECTED**
   - ☐ Matthew 13:22

4. **BEARING GOOD FRUIT IS CONNECTED**
   - ☐ To abiding in Christ
     - ☐ John 15:4-5
   - ☐ To abiding in the Word
     - ☐ John 15:7
   - ☐ To the help of the Holy Spirit
     - ☐ Galatians 5:22-23
     - ☐ Ephesians 5:8-10

5. **BEARING MUCH FRUIT IS PERFECTED**
   - ☐ Through pruning
     - ☐ John 15:2
     - ☐ Hebrews 12:11
     - ☐ Philippians 1:21-22

BEFORE YOU PUT THE SHOVEL DOWN
- ☐ 2 Corinthians 9:10-15

JUNE 27

The Carnal Mind Versus the Mind of Christ *Proverbs 23:7 (NKJV)*

The carnal mind is described as:

1. **DEFILED**
   - ☐ Titus 1:15

2. **DEBASED**
   - ☐ Romans 1:28-29
   - ☐ Psalm 119:115 (NLT)

3. **BLINDED**
   - ☐ 2 Corinthians 3:14; 4:4

4. **CORRUPT**
   - ☐ 2 Corinthians 11:3
   - ☐ 1 Timothy 6:5
   - ☐ 2 Timothy 3:8

5. **DOUBLE-MINDED**
   - ☐ James 1:8
   - ☐ James 4:8
   - ☐ Psalm 119:113

6. **DEATH**
   - ☐ Romans 8:6-7

BEFORE YOU PUT THE SHOVEL DOWN
   - ☐ Ephesians 2:1-3
   - ☐ Ephesians 4:17-19
   - ☐ Colossians 1:21

The Christian mindset is:

1. **CENTERED ON TRUSTING GOD**
   - ☐ Isaiah 26:3

2. **COMMITTED TO LOVING GOD WITH ALL THEIR MIND**
   - ☐ Mark 12:29-30

NOTES

3. **SET ON THINGS ABOVE**
   - ☐ Colossians 3:1-4
   - ☐ Philippians 3:18-19

4. **MODELED AFTER THE MINDSET OF JESUS**
   - ☐ Philippians 2:3-8
   - ☐ 1 Corinthians 2:16
   - ☐ 1 Peter 4:1-2

5. **NOT AFRAID, ANXIOUS OR WORRIED**
   - ☐ Luke 12:22-31
   - ☐ 2 Thessalonians 2:1-2
   - ☐ 2 Timothy 1:7

6. **BEING TRANSFORMED BY CONTINUAL RENEWAL**
   - ☐ Romans 12:2
   - ☐ Ephesians 4:22-24

7. **UNDER THE CONTROL OF THE HOLY SPIRIT**
   - ☐ Romans 8:5-8

8. **ALWAYS PREPARED FOR ACTION**
   - ☐ 1 Peter 1:13 (NLT)
   - ☐ 1 Peter 5:8 (ESV)
   - ☐ Luke 12:35-36 (ESV)

9. **CONVINCED AND CONVICTED BASED ON THE WORD**
   - ☐ Romans 14:5
   - ☐ Acts 17:11

10. **SET ON GLORIFYING GOD**
    - ☐ Romans 15:5-6

BEFORE YOU PUT THE SHOVEL DOWN
- ☐ Philippians 3:15-16
- ☐ Philippians 4:6-9

NOTES

JUNE 28

Seven Reasons Abiding is Absolutely Essential *John 15:1-10 (NKJV)*

Because when we abide in Him:

1. **HE ABIDES IN US**
   - ☐ John 15:4-5
   - ☐ John 14:17

2. **HE GIVES US HIS HOLY SPIRIT**
   - ☐ 1 John 4:13

3. **WE CAN BEAR MUCH FRUIT**
   - ☐ John 15:4-5

4. **WE HAVE ACCESS TO ASK GOD ANYTHING**
   - ☐ John 15:7
   - ☐ John 8:31

5. **WE CAN HAVE CONFIDENCE AT HIS APPEARING**
   - ☐ 1 John 2:28
   - ☐ 1 John 3:20-21

6. **HE HELPS US SAY NO TO SIN**
   - ☐ 1 John 3:6-9
   - ☐ 1 John 2:6

7. **WE BECOME SENSITIVE TO THE NEEDS OF OTHERS**
   - ☐ 1 John 3:17

JUNE 29
Four Negative Reactions to the Resurrection (NKJV)

1. **SOME WERE AFRAID**
   ☐ Luke 24:5

2. **SOME DIDN'T BELIEVE**
   ☐ Luke 24:9-11

3. **SOME DOUBTED**
   ☐ John 20:24-29

4. **SOME WERE DISAPPOINTED**
   ☐ Luke 24:21

JUNE 30
What to Do When Everything is Falling Apart *Psalm 55:11 (NLT)*

1. **I WILL CALL ON THE LORD**
   ☐ Psalm 55:16

2. **I TRUST THE LORD TO SAVE ME**
   ☐ Psalm 55:23
   ☐ Psalm 56:3

3. **I WILL GIVE MY BURDENS TO THE LORD**
   ☐ Psalm 55:22

BEFORE YOU PUT THE SHOVEL DOWN
   ☐ Psalm 119:105-112
   ☐ 2 Corinthians 4:16-18

JULY

JULY 1

Three Commands for Christians Regarding the World
2 Corinthians 6:17 (NKJV)

1. **DO NOT LOVE THE WORLD**
   - ☐ 1 John 2:15-16
   - ☐ 2 Timothy 4:10
   - ☐ James 1:27
   - ☐ James 4:4

2. **DO NOT CONFORM TO THE WORLD**
   - ☐ Romans 12:2

3. **DO NOT BE OF THE WORLD**
   - ☐ John 8:23
   - ☐ John 15:18-19
   - ☐ 1 Peter 4:3-4
   - ☐ John 17:14-17

JULY 2

Ananias and Sapphira *Acts 5:1-11 (NKJV)*

1. **PRIDE**
   - ☐ Acts 5:1-2
   - ☐ Matthew 23:28

2. **LIED**
   - ☐ Acts 5:3-4

3. **DENIED**
   - ☐ Acts 5:8

4. **DIED**
   - ☐ Acts 5:5,10
   - ☐ James 1:15

JULY 3
The Works of the Lord
Psalm 111 (NKJV)

The works of the Lord are:

1. **GREAT**
   - [ ] Psalm 111:2

2. **HONORABLE**
   - [ ] Psalm 111:3

3. **GLORIOUS**
   - [ ] Psalm 111:3

4. **REMARKABLE**
   - [ ] Psalm 111:4

5. **POWERFUL**
   - [ ] Psalm 111:6

6. **TRUTH**
   - [ ] Psalm 111:7

7. **JUSTICE**
   - [ ] Psalm 111:7

8. **SURE**
   - [ ] Psalm 111:7

9. **STEADFAST**
   - [ ] Psalm 111:8

10. **FOREVER**
    - [ ] Psalm 111:8

NOTES

JULY 4

Your Freedom [NLT]

Don't use your freedom:

1. **TO SATISFY YOUR SINFUL FLESH**
   - ☐ Galatians 5:13a

2. **AS AN EXCUSE TO DO EVIL**
   - ☐ 1 Peter 2:16

3. **TO CAUSE OTHERS TO STUMBLE**
   - ☐ 1 Corinthians 8:9

Use your freedom:

1. **TO SERVE ONE ANOTHER IN LOVE**
   - ☐ Galatians 5:13b

2. **TO BE FREE FROM THE LAW**
   - ☐ Galatians 4:11-12

JULY 5

Polluted Christian Living

Zephaniah 3:1-2 (NKJV)

Charges against Jerusalem:

1. **DID NOT OBEY HIS VOICE**
   - ☐ Zephaniah 3:2

2. **DID NOT RECEIVE CORRECTION**
   - ☐ Zephaniah 3:2

3. **DID NOT TRUST IN THE LORD**
   - ☐ Zephaniah 3:2

4. **DID NOT DRAW NEAR GOD**
   - ☐ Zephaniah 3:2

BEFORE YOU PUT THE SHOVEL DOWN
- ☐ James 4:8

JULY 6

Four Stages of Spiritual Growth *John 9:1-41 (NKJV)*

1. **AWARENESS**
   ☐ John 9:11

2. **ACADEMIC**
   ☐ John 9:17

3. **ACKNOWLEDGEMENT**
   ☐ John 9:33

4. **ACCEPTANCE**
   ☐ John 9:35-38

JULY 7

Five Invitations of Christ (NKJV)

1. **COME TO ME**
   ☐ Matthew 11:28

2. **FOLLOW ME**
   ☐ Matthew 4:19

3. **TARRY WITH ME**
   ☐ Luke 24:49

4. **WATCH WITH ME**
   ☐ Matthew 26:38

5. **GO FOR ME**
   ☐ Mark 16:15

NOTES

JULY 8

The Cost of Calvary *Matthew 26 (NKJV)*

1. **GREAT SORROW**
   - ☐ Matthew 26:38

2. **HIS OWN WILL**
   - ☐ Matthew 26:39

3. **INTENSE PRAYER**
   - ☐ Matthew 26:44
   - ☐ Luke 22:44

4. **BETRAYAL**
   - ☐ Peter
     - ☐ Matthew 26:33-34
     - ☐ Matthew 26:69-75
   - ☐ Judas
     - ☐ Matthew 26:47-48
   - ☐ Sinners
     - ☐ Matthew 26:45

5. **INJUSTICE**
   - ☐ Matthew 26:59-62

6. **PHYSICAL PAIN**
   - ☐ Matthew 27:27-35

7. **MOCKERY**
   - ☐ Matthew 26:68
   - ☐ Matthew 27:29-44

JULY 9
Two Ways of Life (NKJV)

1. **A WAY**
   - ☐ Proverbs 12:15
   - ☐ Proverbs 12:26
   - ☐ Proverbs 14:12
   - ☐ Proverbs 16:2
   - ☐ Proverbs 16:25

2. **THE WAY**
   - ☐ John 14:6
   - ☐ Acts 4:12

JULY 10
Two Kinds of Death *Romans 7-8 (NKJV)*

1. **DEATH BY SIN**
   - ☐ Romans 5:12
   - ☐ Romans 6:23
   - ☐ James 1:15

2. **DEATH TO SIN**
   - ☐ Romans 5:12
   - ☐ Colossians 3:5-6
   - ☐ Romans 8:13
   - ☐ Galatians 5:24

NOTES

JULY 11

10 Descriptions of the Wicked
Psalm 10 (NKJV)

1. **HE HUNTS DOWN THE WEAK**
   ☐ Psalm 10:3

2. **HE BOASTS IN THE CRAVINGS OF HIS HEART**
   ☐ Psalm 10:3

3. **HE BLESSES THE GREEDY AND REVILES THE LORD**
   ☐ Psalm 10:3

4. **HE HAS NO ROOM FOR GOD**
   ☐ Psalm 10:4

5. **HE IS FAR FROM GOD'S LAWS**
   ☐ Psalm 10:5

6. **HE THINKS HE IS UNSHAKABLE**
   ☐ Psalm 10:6

7. **HIS MOUTH IS FULL OF TROUBLE**
   ☐ Psalm 10:7

8. **HE LIES IN WAIT LIKE A LION**
   ☐ Psalm 10:9

9. **HE THINKS GOD IS BLIND**
   ☐ Psalm 10:11

10. **HE THINKS HE WILL NOT HAVE TO GIVE AN ACCOUNT TO GOD**
    ☐ Psalm 10:13

NOTES

JULY 12
Our Relationship With Christ
1 Corinthians 4 (NKJV)

1. **FAITHFUL TO CHRIST**
   - ☐ 1 Corinthians 4:2
   - ☐ Matthew 24:45
   - ☐ Matthew 25:21-23
   - ☐ Galatians 5:22

2. **FOOLS FOR CHRIST**
   - ☐ 1 Corinthians 4:10
   - ☐ 1 Corinthians 1:18,23
   - ☐ 1 Corinthians 3:18

3. **FOLLOWERS OF CHRIST**
   - ☐ 1 Corinthians 4:16-17
   - ☐ Galatians 2:20
   - ☐ 1 Corinthians 11:1

JULY 13
God's Grace Romans *5:20-21 (NKJV)*

1. **GIFT FROM GOD**
   - ☐ Ephesians 2:8-9

2. **RELIABLE**
   - ☐ 2 Corinthians 12:9-10

3. **ABUNDANT**
   - ☐ 1 Timothy 1:14

4. **CAME THROUGH CHRIST**
   - ☐ John 1:17

5. **EFFECTIVE**
   - ☐ 1 Corinthians 15:10

NOTES

JULY 14

Paul's Five Key "I" Statements in Philippians *Philippians 3-4 (NIV)*

1. **I CONSIDER EVERYTHING LOSS**
   - ☐ Philippians 3:8-9

2. **I WANT TO KNOW CHRIST**
   - ☐ Philippians 3:10-11

3. **I PRESS ON**
   - ☐ Philippians 3:12-15

4. **I AM CONTENT**
   - ☐ Philippians 4:11-12

5. **I CAN DO ALL THINGS THROUGH CHRIST**
   - ☐ Philippians 4:13

JULY 15

Seven Biblical Practices Great Leaders Follow (NIV)

1. **FOLLOW IN THE FOOTSTEPS OF CHRIST**
   - ☐ 1 Peter 2:21
   - ☐ Psalm 119:14

2. **FOLLOW IN THE FOOTSTEPS OF FAITH**
   - ☐ Romans 4:12
   - ☐ Hebrews 11

3. **FOLLOW IN THE PATTERN OF THOSE WHO HAVE GONE BEFORE US**
   - ☐ Philippians 3:17

4. **FOLLOW GOD'S INSTRUCTION AND DIRECTION**
   - ☐ 1 Timothy 4:6

5. **FOLLOW IN HUMILITY**
   ☐ Galatians 6:13-16

6. **FOLLOW IN THE WAY OF LOVE**
   ☐ 1 Corinthians 14:1
   ☐ John 13:35

7. **FOLLOW PEACE WITH ALL PEOPLE**
   ☐ Romans 14:19 (KJV)
   ☐ Hebrews 12:14 (KJV)

JULY 16
God's Word on Not Giving Up
2 Corinthians 4:8 (NIV)

1. **BE STRONG AND DON'T GIVE UP**
   ☐ 2 Chronicles 15:7

2. **PRAY AND DON'T GIVE UP**
   ☐ Luke 18:1

3. **DO GOOD AND DON'T GIVE UP**
   ☐ Galatians 6:9

4. **CONTINUE MEETING TOGETHER AND DON'T GIVE UP**
   ☐ Hebrews 10:25

5. **DON'T GIVE UP WHEN YOU ARE CORRECTED**
   ☐ Hebrews 12:5 (NLT)

JULY 17

Five Things We Are to Make Every Effort (NIV)

1. ENTER THROUGH THE NARROW DOOR
- ☐ Luke 13:24
- ☐ Matthew 7:13-14
- ☐ Hebrews 4:11

2. DO WHAT LEADS TO PEACE AND HOLINESS
- ☐ Romans 14:19
- ☐ Luke 12:58 (NKJV)
- ☐ Romans 12:18
- ☐ Hebrews 12:14

3. KEEP THE UNITY OF THE SPIRIT
- ☐ Ephesians 4:3
- ☐ Ephesians 4:11-13

4. ADD TO YOUR FAITH
- ☐ 2 Peter 1:5

5. BE FOUND SPOTLESS
- ☐ 2 Peter 3:11-14

BEFORE YOU PUT THE SHOVEL DOWN
- ☐ Philippians 3:12 (HCSB)
- ☐ 2 Peter 1:10 (HCSB)

JULY 18

Those Who Will Find Themselves in the Lake of Fire *Revelation 21:1-8 (NKJV)*

1. COWARDLY
2. UNBELIEVING
3. ABOMINABLE

4. MURDERS
5. SEXUAL IMMORAL
6. SORCERERS
7. IDOLATERS
8. LIARS

Look up and write down Scriptures for each of these groups.

JULY 19
The Secret to Staying Strong in Life's Struggles *Psalm 13:1-6 (NIV)*

How the apostle Paul handled his struggles:

1. **HE PROMOTED THE IMPORTANCE OF PRAYER**
   - ☐ Romans 15:30
   - ☐ Colossians 4:12 (ESV)
   - ☐ Philippians 4:6-7

2. **HE UNDERSTOOD WHO HIS STRUGGLE WAS AGAINST**
   - ☐ Ephesians 6:11-13

3. **HE RECOGNIZED SIMILAR STRUGGLES IN OTHERS**
   - ☐ Philippians 1:29-30
   - ☐ Philippians 2:4

4. **HE ACCEPTED THE FACT THAT STRUGGLES DO NOT ALWAYS GO AWAY**
   - ☐ Philippians 1:30
   - ☐ 1 Timothy 4:10 (NLT)
   - ☐ 1 Peter 5:10 (NKJV)

NOTES

5. HIS STRUGGLE WAS DEPENDENT ON THE SPIRIT OF CHRIST AND NOT HIS OWN
- [ ] Colossians 1:29 (NLT)
- [ ] Zechariah 4:6
- [ ] 2 Corinthians 1:9
- [ ] 2 Corinthians 3:5
- [ ] 2 Corinthians 4:7

6. HE EQUATED THE GREAT PRICE WITH A GREAT PURPOSE
- [ ] Colossians 2:1-3 (ESV)
- [ ] Romans 8:28

7. HE KEPT HIS STRUGGLES IN PERSPECTIVE
- [ ] Hebrews 12:4
- [ ] Romans 8:18

JULY 20

Six Observations About Sanctification
1 Thessalonians 5:23-25 (NKJV)

1. SANCTIFICATION IS SOMETHING GOD CALLS YOU TO
- [ ] 1 Thessalonians 5:24
- [ ] 1 Thessalonians 4:3
- [ ] 1 Peter 1:15-16

2. SANCTIFICATION IS SOMETHING THAT CAN HAPPEN NOW
- [ ] 1 Thessalonians 5:23

3. SANCTIFICATION IS A WORK ONLY GOD CAN DO
- [ ] 1 Thessalonians 5:23-24
- [ ] John 17:17
- [ ] Ephesians 5:26
- [ ] 1 Corinthians 1:30
- [ ] Hebrews 2:11

4. SANCTIFICATION IS A COMPLETE WORK
- [ ] 1 Thessalonians 5:23

5. **SANCTIFICATION IS SOMETHING THAT IS PROGRESSIVE AND ONGOING**
   - ☐ 1 Thessalonians 5:23
   - ☐ 1 Corinthians 1:8-9
   - ☐ 1 Thessalonians 3:11-13

6. **SANCTIFICATION DEMANDS A LOT OF PRAYER AND GRACE**
   - ☐ 1 Thessalonians 5:17,25
   - ☐ Three keys to this grace:
     - ☐ Pray without ceasing
       (*1 Thessalonians 5:17*)
     - ☐ Avoid the appearance of evil
       (*1 Thessalonians 5:19*)
     - ☐ Grace of God with us
       (*1 Thessalonians 5:22*)

JULY 21
Holiness (NKJV)

The Bible commands us to:

1. **PARTAKE IN HOLINESS**
   - ☐ Hebrews 12:10

2. **PURSUE HOLINESS**
   - ☐ Hebrews 12:14

3. **PRACTICE HOLINESS**
   - ☐ 1 John 2:28-29
   - ☐ 1 John 3:7

4. **PERFECT HOLINESS**
   - ☐ 2 Corinthians 7:1

JULY 22

Three Things Must Happen in the Life of Every Disciple *Luke 9:21-22 (NLT)*

1. TAKE OFF SELFISH AMBITION
☐ Galatians 5:20

2. TAKE UP THE CROSS
☐ Galatians 2:20
☐ Galatians 6:14

3. TAKE ON AND FOLLOW CHRIST
☐ Matthew 4:19
☐ Luke 14:27
☐ Matthew 10:38
☐ Luke 9:57-62

JULY 23

Everyone Involved in Missions
Mark 16:15-20 (NLT)

"Lord, give me a greater ambition for the Great Commission."

Five observations that simplify the Great Commission:

1. THE GOSPEL IS FOR EVERYONE
☐ Mark 16:15
☐ Revelation 5:9
☐ Philippians 2:10-11
☐ Romans 3:23
☐ Romans 1:16

2. **THE GOSPEL MUST BE SHARED EVERYWHERE**
   - ☐ Mark 16:15-20
   - ☐ Acts 1:8
   - ☐ Acts 10:42
   - ☐ Acts 17:30
   - ☐ Romans 1:5
   - ☐ Romans 16:26

3. **THE GOSPEL IS THE RESPONSIBILITY OF EVERYBODY**

4. **THE GOSPEL REQUIRES OUR EVERYTHING**
   - ☐ Luke 5:27
   - ☐ Matthew 19:27
   - ☐ Acts 2:44
   - ☐ 1 Corinthians 9:22

5. **THE GOSPEL IS AN EVERYDAY EVENT**
   - ☐ Acts 5:42
   - ☐ Acts 16:5
   - ☐ Ephesians 3:9

JULY 24
If You Do This (NLT)

- ☐ Deuteronomy 30:16
- ☐ 1 Kings 2:4
- ☐ Proverbs 3:2
- ☐ Acts 15:29
- ☐ Exodus 18:23 (NKJV)
- ☐ Numbers 32:20 (NKJV)

NOTES

JULY 25
God is Attracted to Weakness (NKJV)

- [ ] Judges 6:15
- [ ] Zechariah 4:1-6
- [ ] 2 Corinthians 12:9-10
- [ ] Hebrews 11:34
- [ ] 1 Corinthians 1:27
- [ ] Romans 8:26
- [ ] Hebrews 4:15
- [ ] Isaiah 40:29
- [ ] Joel 3:10
- [ ] Isaiah 35:3

JULY 26
Postures of Prayer in the Bible (NKJV)

1. **STANDING**
   - [ ] 1 Samuel 1:26
   - [ ] John 11:41
   - [ ] Luke 18:10-14
   - [ ] 2 Chronicles 20:13

2. **LIFTING OR STRETCHING OUT YOUR HANDS**
   - [ ] 1 Timothy 2:8
   - [ ] Psalm 141:2
   - [ ] Exodus 9:29

3. **LIFTING YOUR EYES TOWARD HEAVEN**
   - [ ] Psalm 121:1
   - [ ] Mark 6:41
   - [ ] Luke 9:16
   - [ ] John 11:41
   - [ ] John 17:1

4. **SITTING**
   - ☐ 2 Samuel 7:18
   - ☐ Judges 20:26-27

5. **LYING IN BED**
   - ☐ Psalm 4:4
   - ☐ Psalm 63:6

6. **BOWING**
   - ☐ Exodus 34:8
   - ☐ 1 Kings 18:42
   - ☐ 2 Chronicles 20:18
   - ☐ Nehemiah 8:6
   - ☐ Psalm 5:7

7. **PROSTRATE ON YOUR FACE**
   - ☐ Genesis 17:3
   - ☐ Joshua 7:6
   - ☐ Revelation 1:17
   - ☐ Matthew 26:39
   - ☐ Revelation 5:8-14

8. **KNEELING**
   - ☐ 2 Chronicles 6:13
   - ☐ Ezra 9:5
   - ☐ Psalm 95:6
   - ☐ Daniel 6:10
   - ☐ Luke 22:41-42
   - ☐ Acts 9:40
   - ☐ Acts 20:36
   - ☐ Ephesians 3:14

9. **WALKING**
   - ☐ Genesis 13:14-17
   - ☐ Joshua 6:1-21

NOTES

JULY 27
Three Responses to the Devil (NKJV)

1. **REFUSE**
   - ☐ Ephesians 4:27

2. **RESIST**
   - ☐ James 4:7
   - ☐ 1 Peter 5:8-9

3. **REBUKE**
   - ☐ Matthew 4:10-11
   - ☐ Romans 16:20
   - ☐ Revelation 12:11

JULY 28
Powerful Prayers *James 5 (NKJV)*

1. **PRAYER OF FAITHFULNESS**
   - ☐ James 5:13-14

2. **PRAYER OF FAITH**
   - ☐ James 5:15

3. **PRAYER OF FERVENCY**
   - ☐ James 5:16

4. **PRAYER OF FAULTLESSNESS**
   - ☐ James 5:16b

JULY 29
The Seven Excepts in the Bible [KJV]

1. **EXCEPT YOU REPENT**
   ☐ Luke 13:1-5

2. **EXCEPT YOU BE CONVERTED**
   ☐ Matthew 18:3

3. **EXCEPT A MAN BE BORN AGAIN**
   ☐ John 3:3

4. **EXCEPT YOU BE BORN OF WATER AND SPIRIT**
   ☐ John 3:5

5. **EXCEPT YOU EAT THE FLESH**
   ☐ John 6:53

6. **EXCEPT YOUR RIGHTEOUSNESS EXCEEDS**
   ☐ Matthew 5:20

7. **EXCEPT YOU ABIDE IN ME**
   ☐ John 15:4-6

JULY 30
The Four Things God Does After You Suffer Awhile *1 Peter 5:10 (NLT)*

1. **RESTORE YOU**
   ☐ 1 Peter 5:10

2. **SUPPORT YOU**
   ☐ 1 Peter 5:10

3. **STRENGTHEN YOU**
   - ☐ 1 Peter 5:10

4. **PLACE YOU ON SOLID FOUNDATION**
   - ☐ 2 Corinthians 4:17
   - ☐ James 1:12
   - ☐ 1 Peter 1:6-7
   - ☐ Romans 5:3-5
   - ☐ Romans 8:18
   - ☐ Psalm 138:7

JULY 31

Six Basic Beliefs *Mark 1:14-18 (NKJV)*

We must believe:

1. **GOD EXISTS**
   - ☐ John 5:24
   - ☐ Acts 16:34
   - ☐ Hebrews 11:6
   - ☐ 1 Peter 1:21

2. **IN GOD'S WORD**
   - ☐ John 2:22
   - ☐ John 20:31
   - ☐ 2 Timothy 3:16

3. **JESUS CHRIST IS THE SON OF GOD**
   - ☐ Matthew 21:32
   - ☐ John 3:15-18
   - ☐ John 6:29
   - ☐ John 8:24
   - ☐ John 14:1
   - ☐ Acts 8:37
   - ☐ 1 John 5:4-5,10

4. **JESUS DIED AND ROSE AGAIN**
   - ☐ Matthew 28:6
   - ☐ Romans 10:9-10
   - ☐ 1 Corinthians 15:3-4,20
   - ☐ John 11:25

5. **THERE IS FORGIVENESS IN HIS NAME**
   - ☐ John 1:12
   - ☐ Acts 4:12
   - ☐ Acts 10:43
   - ☐ Acts 13:39
   - ☐ Philippians 2:10
   - ☐ 1 John 3:23

6. **WE WILL SPEND ETERNITY WITH CHRIST IF WE LIVE FOR HIM**
   - ☐ John 3:36
   - ☐ John 11:26
   - ☐ Romans 6:8
   - ☐ 1 Thessalonians 4:14
   - ☐ 1 Timothy 1:16

AUGUST

AUGUST 1

It's Worth Repeating, "Love Your Neighbor as Yourself" (NKJV)

- ☐ Leviticus 19:18
- ☐ Matthew 19:19
- ☐ Matthew 22:39-40
- ☐ Mark 12:31-34
- ☐ Luke 10:27-37
- ☐ Romans 13:9
- ☐ Galatians 5:14
- ☐ James 2:8
- ☐ Matthew 5:43-44

AUGUST 2

Four Important Words in Your Spiritual Journey (NKJV)

1. **COME**
   - ☐ Matthew 11:28-29
   - ☐ John 6:37
   - ☐ John 7:37
   - ☐ John 14:6

2. **BECOME**
   - ☐ John 1:12-13
   - ☐ Mark 1:17
   - ☐ 1 Corinthians 9:22

3. **OVERCOME**
   - ☐ John 16:33
   - ☐ 1 John 2:13-14
   - ☐ 1 John 5:4-5
   - ☐ Romans 12:21

4. **OUTCOME**
   - ☐ Hebrews 13:7
   - ☐ 1 Peter 1:9 (ESV)

AUGUST 3

Do Everything Acts 13:22 (NLT)

1. **IN LOVE**
   ☐ 1 Corinthians 16:14

2. **WITHOUT COMPLAINING**
   ☐ Philippians 2:14

3. **THROUGH CHRIST**
   ☐ Philippians 4:13

4. **POSSIBLE TO HELP OTHERS**
   ☐ Titus 3:13

5. **IN THE NAME OF THE LORD**
   ☐ Colossians 3:17 (AMP)

AUGUST 4

The Seven Blessings Revealed in Revelation (NKJV)

☑ Revelation 1:3
☐ Revelation 14:13
☐ Revelation 16:15
☐ Revelation 19:9
☐ Revelation 20:6
☐ Revelation 22:7
☐ Revelation 22:14

Handwritten notes: Rev 1:3 is what I read today so I know the time of God is near, so act like God is coming everyday.

NOTES

I read Psalm 35:25 all who are against the Lord will face his wrath when he is judgd

AUGUST 5
What Does the Bible Have to Say About Marriage? (NKJV)

- ☐ Genesis 1:28
- ☐ Genesis 2:18-23
- ☐ Genesis 2:24
- ☐ Proverbs 18:22
- ☐ Ecclesiastes 4:9-12
- ☐ Malachi 2:14
- ☐ Matthew 19:5-6
- ☐ Mark 10:7
- ☐ John 2:1-11
- ☐ Romans 7:2-3
- ☐ 1 Corinthians 7:10-11
- ☐ 1 Corinthians 13:4-13
- ☐ 2 Corinthians 6:14-16
- ☐ Hebrews 13:4-5

AUGUST 6
Four Things to Stir Up (NKJV)

1. **YOURSELF**
   - ☑ Psalm 35:23

2. **THE GIFT OF GOD**
   - ☐ 2 Timothy 1:6

3. **LOVE AND GOOD WORKS**
   - ☐ Hebrews 10:24

4. **PURE MINDS**
   - ☐ 2 Peter 3:1

AUGUST 7

Seven Ways We Should Live As (NIV)

1. **BELIEVERS**
   ☐ 1 John 2:6

2. **CHILDREN OF THE LIGHT**
   ☐ Ephesians 5:8

3. **CITIZENS OF HEAVEN**
   ☑ Philippians 1:27 (NLT)

4. **GOD'S OBEDIENT CHILDREN**
   ☐ 1 Peter 1:14 (NLT)

5. **STRANGERS**
   ☐ 1 Peter 1:17

6. **FREE MEN**
   ☐ 1 Peter 2:16

7. **JESUS DID**
   ☐ 1 John 2:6

AUGUST 8

May I Never Forget *Psalm 103:1-5 (NLT)*

1. **HE FORGIVES ALL MY SIN**
   ☑ Psalm 103:3,12

2. **HE HEALS ALL MY DISEASES**
   ☐ Psalm 103:3

3. **HE REDEEMS MY LIFE FROM DEATH**
   ☐ Psalm 103:4

Notes:

I read Philippians 1:27 act like God is coming every day.

I read Psalm 103:3,12 it says God forgaives all iniquity.

4. **HE CROWNS ME WITH LOVE AND TENDER MERCY**
      - ☐ Psalm 103:4

   5. **HE FILLS MY LIFE WITH GOOD THINGS**
      - ☐ Psalm 103:5

AUGUST 9
Four Things Pride Leads To (NLT)

1. **SHAME AND DISGRACE**
   - ☐ Proverbs 11:2

2. **CONFLICT AND STRIFE**
   - ☐ Proverbs 13:10

3. **DESTRUCTION**
   - ☐ Proverbs 16:18
   - ☐ Proverbs 18:12

4. **HUMILIATION**
   - ☐ Proverbs 29:23

AUGUST 10
Prescription for Spiritual Victory (NLT)

1. **PRAY THREE TIMES A DAY**
   - ☐ Daniel 6:10-13

2. **PRAISE SEVEN TIMES A DAY**
   - ☐ Psalm 119:164

3. **FORGIVE SEVEN TIMES A DAY**
   - ☐ Luke 17:1-5
   - ☐ Matthew 18:21-22

AUGUST 11
The Lord is Close (NLT)

1. **TO THE BROKENHEARTED**
   ☑ Psalm 34:18

2. **TO THOSE WHO CALL ON HIM**
   ☐ Psalm 145:18

3. **TO THOSE WHO TRUST IN HIM**
   ☐ Nahum 1:7

AUGUST 12
Note Those *Luke 13:30 (NLT)*

1. **WHO CAUSE DIVISION**
   ☐ Romans 16:17 (NKJV)

2. **WHO REFUSE TO OBEY**
   ☐ 2 Thessalonians 3:14 (NKJV)

3. **WHO WALK IN GODLY EXAMPLE**
   ☐ Philippians 3:17 (NKJV)

BEFORE YOU PUT THE SHOVEL DOWN
☐ Acts 4:13 (NIV)
☐ Romans 11:22 (ESV)

NOTES

I read psalm 34:18 and reading it I now know God is close to me always wither I follow him or is broken hearted.

AUGUST 13
Biblical Instruction for Husbands (NKJV)

- [ ] Deuteronomy 24:5
- [ ] Proverbs 5:18-19
- [ ] Proverbs 12:4
- [ ] Proverbs 31:10-11,28
- [ ] Ecclesiastes 9:9
- [ ] Malachi 2:14-15
- [ ] 1 Corinthians 7:1-8
- [ ] 1 Corinthians 14:35
- [ ] Ephesians 5:23-28
- [ ] Colossians 3:19
- [ ] 1 Timothy 5:8
- [ ] 1 Peter 3:7

AUGUST 14
Biblical Instruction for Wives (NKJV)

- [ ] Genesis 2:18-20
- [ ] Esther 1:20
- [ ] Proverbs 5:19
- [ ] 1 Corinthians 7:1-8
- [ ] Proverbs 12:4
- [ ] Proverbs 31:10-31
- [ ] Malachi 2:14-15
- [ ] Ephesians 5:22
- [ ] Colossians 3:18
- [ ] 1 Peter 3:5
- [ ] 1 Timothy 3:11
- [ ] Titus 2:4

AUGUST 15

What the Bible Teaches About Sex Before Marriage (NKJV)

1. **ABSTAIN FROM SEXUAL IMMORALITY**
   - ☐ 1 Thessalonians 4:3
   - ☐ Acts 15:20

2. **WE SHOULD FLEE SEXUAL IMMORALITY**
   - ☐ 1 Corinthians 6:18

3. **SHOULD NOT BE A HINT OF SEXUAL IMMORALITY**
   - ☐ Ephesians 5:3

4. **STOP ANY FORM OF SEXUAL IMMORALITY**
   - ☒ Colossians 3:5

5. **SHOULD BE SAVED FOR WEDDING DAY**
   - ☐ Hebrews 13:4

6. **DON'T SELL OUT FOR A MOMENT OF PLEASURE**
   - ☐ Hebrews 12:16

7. **GOD WILL JUDGE THOSE WHO ARE IMMORAL**
   - ☐ Hebrews 13:4

8. **THOSE WHO PRACTICE SEXUAL SIN SHALL NOT SHARE IN THE KINGDOM OF GOD**
   - ☐ 1 Corinthians 6:9-10
   - ☐ Galatians 5:19-20

9. **IF YOU ARE SEXUALLY ACTIVE, STOP AND REPENT**
   - ☐ 2 Corinthians 12:21

NOTES

I read Colossians 3:5 today. Put to death all sexual immorality and resist its temptations

I Read Exodus 20:14.
Do not comet adultry.

AUGUST 16
What the Bible Teaches About Sex After Marriage (NKJV)

1. **GOD CREATED IT**
   ☐ Genesis 1:28-31

2. **IT IS GOOD AND PLEASING**
   ☐ Genesis 2:24-25

3. **IS THE PLACE FOR SEXUAL SATISFACTION**
   ☐ Proverbs 5:15-19

4. **SHOULD NOT DEPRIVE ONE ANOTHER**
   ☐ 1 Corinthians 7:3-5

5. **SHALL NOT COMMIT ADULTERY**
   ☒ Exodus 20:14
   ☐ Proverbs 6:32

6. **THE MARRIAGE BED IS TO BE KEPT PURE**
   ☐ Hebrews 13:4

7. **INTENDED TO REPRODUCE CHILDREN**
   ☐ Psalm 127:3-5

AUGUST 17
Those Who Will Not Inherit the Kingdom of God (NIV)

☐ 1 Corinthians 6:9-11
☐ 1 Corinthians 15:50
☐ Galatians 5:19-21
☐ Ephesians 5:4-5
☐ James 2:5

NOTES

AUGUST 18

Five Things the Bible Has to Say About Anger *Matthew 5:21-26 (NLT)*

1. **WE SHOULD BE SLOW TO GET ANGRY**
   - ☐ James 1:19-20
   - ☐ Proverbs 14:17,29
   - ☐ Proverbs 15:18
   - ☐ Proverbs 16:32 (NKJV)
   - ☐ Proverbs 19:11

2. **WE SHOULD AVOID THOSE WHO ARE ANGRY**
   - ☐ Proverbs 22:24
   - ☐ Proverbs 29:22

3. **WE SHOULD NOT SIN IN OUR ANGER**
   - ☐ Ephesians 4:26-27
   - ☐ Psalm 4:4
   - ☐ Galatians 5:19-21

4. **WE CAN SETTLE OUR ANGER QUICKER**
   - ☐ Ephesians 4:26
   - ☐ Jeremiah 3:12

5. **WE CAN BE SMARTER ABOUT HOW OUR ACTIONS MIGHT MAKE SOMEONE ANGRY**
   - ☐ Proverbs 15:1
   - ☐ Proverbs 20:2
   - ☐ Proverbs 10:12

BEFORE YOU PUT THE SHOVEL DOWN
- ☐ 2 Corinthians 12:20-21
- ☐ Psalm 37:8
- ☐ Ecclesiastes 7:9
- ☐ Colossians 3:5-8
- ☐ Ephesians 4:30-31
- ☐ 1 Timothy 2:8

AUGUST 19
"If We Say" Statements *1 John (NKJV)*

- [ ] 1 John 1:6
- [ ] 1 John 1:8
- [ ] 1 John 1:10
- [ ] 1 John 2:1-4
- [ ] 1 John 2:6
- [ ] 1 John 2:9
- [ ] 1 John 4:20

AUGUST 20
The "If . . . Then" Clauses
1 John (NKJV)

- [ ] 1 John 1:6
- [ ] 1 John 1:7
- [ ] 1 John 1:9
- [ ] 1 John 1:10
- [ ] 1 John 2:1
- [ ] 1 John 2:3
- [ ] 1 John 2:15
- [ ] 1 John 2:19
- [ ] 1 John 2:24
- [ ] 1 John 2:29
- [ ] 1 John 3:21
- [ ] 1 John 4:11
- [ ] 1 John 4:12
- [ ] 1 John 4:20
- [ ] 1 John 5:9
- [ ] 1 John 5:14

NOTES

AUGUST 21
What the Bible Has to Say About Fellowship (NKJV)

1. **WE ARE NOT TO CLAIM TO HAVE FELLOWSHIP IF WE DON'T HAVE IT**
   - ☐ 1 John 1:6

2. **WE ARE NOT TO HAVE FELLOWSHIP WITH THE WORLD**
   - ☐ Ephesians 5:11
   - ☐ 1 John 1:7
   - ☐ 2 Corinthians 6:14

3. **WE ARE CALLED TO HAVE FELLOWSHIP WITH CHRIST**
   - ☐ 1 Corinthians 1:9
   - ☐ 1 John 1:3
   - ☐ Philippians 2:11
   - ☐ Philippians 3:10

4. **WE NEED THE FELLOWSHIP OF OTHER BELIEVERS**
   - ☐ Acts 2:42

5. **WE CAN EXPERIENCE THE FELLOWSHIP OF THE HOLY SPIRIT**
   - ☐ 2 Corinthians 13:14 (NIV)

AUGUST 22
Biblical Definitions of Sin (NKJV)

1. **ALL UNRIGHTEOUSNESS = SIN**
   - ☐ 1 John 5:17

2. **LAWLESSNESS = SIN**
   - ☐ 1 John 3:4

3. **SHOWING PARTIALITY = SIN**
   - ☐ James 2:9-11

NOTES

4. **KNOWING TO DO GOOD AND NOT DOING IT = SIN**
   - ☐ James 4:17

5. **WILLFUL DISOBEDIENCE TO THE KNOWN WILL OF GOD = SIN**
   - ☐ Hebrews 10:26-29

6. **WHATEVER IS NOT OF FAITH = SIN**
   - ☐ Romans 14:23

AUGUST 23

Five Responsibilities Toward Those We See Sinning (NKJV)

1. **PRAY FOR THAT PERSON**
   - ☐ 1 John 5:16-17
   - ☐ James 5:14-15

2. **GO SHOW HIM HIS FAULT**
   - ☐ Matthew 18:15-17
   - ☐ Ezekiel 3:17-21

3. **THOSE WHO CONTINUE—REBUKE IN PRESENCE OF ALL**
   - ☐ 1 Timothy 5:20

4. **SHARE SCRIPTURE TO INSTRUCT AND CORRECT**
   - ☐ 2 Timothy 3:16-17
   - ☐ Hebrews 3:13

5. **RESTORE AND RETURN**
   - ☐ Galatians 6:1
   - ☐ James 5:19-20

AUGUST 24

The 21 Works of The Devil: [Part 1] *1 John 3:8 (NKJV)*

1. **QUESTION AND PERVERT GOD'S WORD**
   - ☐ Genesis 3:1

2. **INFLICT**
   - ☐ Job 2:7

3. **OPPOSE**
   - ☐ Zechariah 3:1
   - ☐ 2 Corinthians 12:6-7

4. **TEMPT**
   - ☐ Matthew 4:1-3

5. **POSSESS**
   - ☐ Matthew 8:28

6. **SNATCH**
   - ☐ Matthew 13:19

7. **SOW TARES**
   - ☐ Matthew 13:38-39

8. **BIND**
   - ☐ Luke 13:16

9. **SIFT LIKE WHEAT**
   - ☐ Luke 22:31

10. **LIE AND DECEIVE**
    - ☐ John 8:44
    - ☐ 2 Corinthians 11:3-4,14
    - ☐ Revelation 20:7-10

11. **FILL YOUR HEART**
    - ☐ Acts 5:3
    - ☐ John 13:2

AUGUST 25

The 21 Works of The Devil: [Part 2] (NKJV)

12. OPPRESS
- ☐ Acts 10:38

13. BEFRIEND
- ☐ 1 Corinthians 10:20-21
- ☐ Ephesians 5:11

14. BLINDS TO THE TRUTH
- ☐ 2 Corinthians 4:4

15. TORMENT
- ☐ 2 Corinthians 12:6-7

16. HINDERS
- ☐ 1 Thessalonians 2:18

17. TRICK AND TRAP
- ☐ Matthew 16:23
- ☐ 1 Timothy 3:7
- ☐ 2 Timothy 2:26

18. INSTIGATE FALSE DOCTRINE
- ☐ 1 Timothy 4:1-4

19. TAKE CAPTIVE
- ☐ 2 Timothy 2:26

20. DEVOUR AND DESTROY
- ☐ 1 Peter 5:8
- ☐ John 10:10

21. ACCUSE
- ☐ Revelation 12:10

NOTES

AUGUST 26
The Five Old Testament Covenants [NKJV]

1. **THE COVENANT OF ADAM**
   - ☐ Genesis 2:15-17
   - ☐ Hosea 6:7

2. **THE COVENANT OF NOAH**
   - ☐ Genesis 6:18
   - ☐ Isaiah 54:9

3. **THE COVENANT OF ABRAHAM**
   - ☐ Genesis 15:18

4. **THE COVENANT OF MOSES TO ISRAEL**
   - ☐ Exodus 19:5-6

5. **THE COVENANT OF DAVID**
   - ☐ 2 Samuel 23:4-5
   - ☐ 2 Chronicles 7:17-18
   - ☐ 2 Chronicles 13:5
   - ☐ Psalm 89:3
   - ☐ Jeremiah 33:21

AUGUST 27
Six Stewardship Laws [NKJV]

1. **GOD IS THE OWNER**
   - ☐ Psalm 24:1

2. **I AM THE STEWARD**
   - ☐ 1 Corinthians 4:1-2

3. **WE MUST GIVE AN ACCOUNT OF OUR STEWARDSHIP**
   - ☐ Romans 14:10-13
   - ☐ Matthew 25:14-30

4. **I AM RESPONSIBLE**
   - ☐ Luke 12:35-48

5. **IF I AM FAITHFUL, I WILL BE REWARDED**
   ☐ Matthew 25:14-30

6. **IF I AM UNFAITHFUL, I WILL BE PUNISHED**
   ☐ Matthew 25:14-30

AUGUST 28
The Eight Causes of Financial Bondage (NKJV)

1. **LACK OF CONTENTMENT**
   ☐ 1 Timothy 6:6-9

2. **GREED**
   ☐ 1 Timothy 6:10-11

3. **SLOTHFULNESS**
   ☐ 2 Thessalonians 3:6-10
   ☐ 1 Timothy 5:8

4. **LACK OF GENEROSITY**
   ☐ James 2:14-16

5. **WRONG PRIORITIES**
   ☐ Matthew 6:33
   ☐ Proverbs 11:28

6. **NOT HONORING GOD WITH THE TITHE**
   ☐ Malachi 3:6-10

7. **WORLDLINESS**
   ☐ 1 John 2:15-17
   ☐ Matthew 19:16-24

8. **NOT TRUSTING GOD TO SUPPLY ALL OUR NEEDS**
   ☐ Proverbs 3:5-6
   ☐ Philippians 4:19

AUGUST 29
What the Lord Knows About the Righteous *Psalm 1:6 (NKJV)*

He knows:

1. **THOSE WHO ARE HIS**
   - ☐ 2 Timothy 2:19
   - ☐ John 10:14

2. **THE WAY I TAKE**
   - ☐ Job 23:10

3. **THOSE WHO TRUST IN HIM**
   - ☐ Nahum 1:7

4. **THE THOUGHTS OF THE WISE**
   - ☐ 1 Corinthians 3:20
   - ☐ Psalm 94:11

5. **THE DAYS OF THE BLAMELESS**
   - ☐ Psalm 37:18-24

6. **HOW TO DELIVER THE RIGHTEOUS OUT OF TEMPTATION**
   - ☐ 2 Peter 2:9

AUGUST 30
Watch What You Practice
1 John 3:7-10 (NKJV)

- ☐ 1 John 1:6
- ☐ 1 John 2:29
- ☐ 1 John 3:7
- ☐ 1 John 3:10
- ☐ Psalm 141:4
- ☐ Romans 13:4
- ☐ Galatians 5:19-21

AUGUST 31
The "As For Me" Passages [NLT]

- [ ] Joshua 24:15
- [ ] 1 Samuel 12:23
- [ ] Job 19:25
- [ ] Psalm 49:15
- [ ] Psalm 73:28
- [ ] Psalm 75:9
- [ ] Jeremiah 26:14
- [ ] Micah 7:7
- [ ] Galatians 6:14

SEPTEMBER

SEPTEMBER 1

The Message of Missions in the Book of Psalms (NLT)

- [ ] Psalm 2:7-10
- [ ] Psalm 8:9
- [ ] Psalm 9:11-12,17-20
- [ ] Psalm 33:13-14
- [ ] Psalm 40:9-10
- [ ] Psalm 46:10
- [ ] Psalm 48:10
- [ ] Psalm 65:5-8
- [ ] Psalm 67:1-2
- [ ] Psalm 72: 17-19
- [ ] Psalm 79:10
- [ ] Psalm 86:9-10
- [ ] Psalm 96:3
- [ ] Psalm 96:11-13
- [ ] Psalm 97:4-7
- [ ] Psalm 98:2-3
- [ ] Psalm 102:18-22

SEPTEMBER 2

The Impact of Every (NKJV)

1. **EVERY PERSON**
   - [ ] Colossians 1:28

2. **EVERY PLACE**
   - [ ] 1 Corinthians 1:2
   - [ ] 2 Corinthians 2:14
   - [ ] 1 Thessalonians 1:8

3. **EVERY NATION TRIBE AND TONGUE**
   - [ ] Revelation 5:9

4. **EVERY EYE WILL SEE HIM**
   - [ ] Revelation 1:7

5. **EVERY KNEE SHALL BOW**
   - ☐ Philippians 2:10
   - ☐ Romans 14:11

6. **EVERY TONGUE CONFESS**
   - ☐ Philippians 2:9-11

SEPTEMBER 3
Your Faith Can Change the World [NKJV]

1. **YOUR FAITH HAS GONE OUT**
   - ☐ 1 Thessalonians 1:8

2. **YOUR FAITH IS SPOKEN OF THROUGHOUT THE WORLD**
   - ☐ Romans 1:8
   - ☐ Philemon 1:3-6

3. **YOUR FAITH IS BEARING FRUIT**
   - ☐ Ephesians 1:15-16
   - ☐ Colossians 1:3-6

4. **YOUR FAITH IS GROWING**
   - ☐ 2 Corinthians 10:15
   - ☐ 2 Thessalonians 1:3

SEPTEMBER 4
Personal Instructions: [Part 1] [NLT]

1. **SEPARATE YOURSELF**
   - ☐ 2 Corinthians 6:17

2. **EXAMINE YOURSELF**
   - ☐ 2 Corinthians 13:5

3. **CONSIDER YOURSELF**
   - ☐ Galatians 6:1 (NKJV)

NOTES

4. **KEEP YOURSELF**
   ☐ Ephesians 4:3

5. **CONDUCT YOURSELF**
   ☐ Philippians 1:27

SEPTEMBER 5

Personal Instructions: [Part 2] (NLT)

1. **DEVOTE YOURSELF**
   ☐ Colossians 4:2

2. **TRAIN YOURSELF TO GODLINESS**
   ☐ 1 Timothy 4:7

3. **THROW YOURSELF INTO MEDITATING ON GOD'S WORD**
   ☐ 1 Timothy 4:15

4. **TAKE HEED TO YOURSELF**
   ☐ 1 Timothy 4:16 (NKJV)

5. **KEEP YOURSELF PURE**
   ☐ 1 Timothy 5:22

6. **PRESENT YOURSELF**
   ☐ 2 Timothy 2:15

7. **SHOW YOURSELF A PATTERN OF GOOD WORKS**
   ☐ Titus 2:7 (NKJV)

SEPTEMBER 6

The 10 "Stand" Commands in Scripture: [Part 1] *2 Chronicles 29:11 (NKJV)*

1. **STAND**
   - ☐ Ephesians 6:13-14
   - ☐ 1 Peter 5:12

2. **STAND AGAINST**
   - ☐ Ephesians 6:11

3. **STAND CAREFULLY**
   - ☐ 1 Corinthians 10:12

4. **STAND BEFORE**
   - ☐ 1 Kings 10:8
   - ☐ 1 Kings 17:1
   - ☐ 1 Kings 18:15
   - ☐ 1 Kings 19:11

5. **STAND FIRM**
   - ☐ 1 Corinthians 15:1
   - ☐ 1 Corinthians 16:13
   - ☐ 2 Corinthians 1:21-24
   - ☐ Colossians 1:23
   - ☐ 1 Thessalonians 3:6-8

SEPTEMBER 7

The 10 Stand Commands in Scripture: [Part 2] (NKJV)

6. **STAND BY FAITH**
   - ☐ 2 Corinthians 1:24

7. **STAND FAST**
   - ☐ Philippians 1:27
   - ☐ Philippians 4:1

8. STAND STILL
- [ ] Exodus 14:13
- [ ] 2 Chronicles 20:17
- [ ] Numbers 9:8

9. STAND AND SEE
- [ ] 1 Samuel 12:16
- [ ] Luke 21:28 (NLT)

10. STAND PERFECT
- [ ] Colossians 4:12

SEPTEMBER 8
Four Simple Commands (KJV)

1. FRET NOT
- [ ] Psalm 37:1,7-8
- [ ] Proverbs 24:19

2. FAINT NOT
- [ ] 2 Corinthians 4:1,16
- [ ] Galatians 6:9

3. FEAR NOT
- [ ] Genesis 15:1
- [ ] Genesis 21:17
- [ ] Genesis 26:23-24
- [ ] Joshua 8:1
- [ ] Joshua 10:25
- [ ] Matthew 10:28
- [ ] Luke 12:7,32

4. FAIL NOT
- [ ] Luke 22:32
- [ ] Lamentations 3:22

SEPTEMBER 9
David's Favorite Prayer, "Have Mercy on Me" (NKJV)

- [ ] Psalm 4:1
- [ ] Psalm 6:1-2
- [ ] Psalm 9:13
- [ ] Psalm 25:16
- [ ] Psalm 26:11
- [ ] Psalm 27:7
- [ ] Psalm 30:10
- [ ] Psalm 31:9
- [ ] Psalm 41:4,10
- [ ] Psalm 51:1
- [ ] Psalm 57:1
- [ ] Psalm 86:3,16
- [ ] Psalm 116:1
- [ ] Psalm 119:77
- [ ] Psalm 123:3

SEPTEMBER 10
Six Acts That Can Change the World (NIV)

1. ACT OF KINDNESS
- [ ] Acts 4:9

2. ACT OF RIGHTEOUSNESS
- [ ] Romans 5:18

3. ACT OF WORSHIP
- [ ] Romans 12:1 (AMP)

4. ACT OF GRACE
- [ ] 2 Corinthians 8:6

5. ACT OF BELIEVING
- [ ] John 20:30-31 (MSG)

6. ACT OF GIVING
- [ ] 2 Corinthians 8:7 (NLT)

SEPTEMBER 11

The Upheaval of Evil
2 Timothy 3:13 (NKJV)

Some instructions:

1. **DO NOT FOLLOW A CROWD TO DO EVIL**
   - ☐ Exodus 23:2
2. **DO NOT FRET BECAUSE OF EVIL DOERS**
   - ☐ Psalm 37:1
3. **DO NOT INCLINE YOUR HEART TO EVIL**
   - ☐ Psalm 141:4
4. **DO NOT BE WISE IN YOUR OWN EYE . . . DEPART FROM EVIL**
   - ☐ Proverbs 3:7
5. **DO NOT DEVISE EVIL**
   - ☐ Proverbs 3:29
6. **DO NOT ENTER THE PATH OF THE EVIL**
   - ☐ Proverbs 4:14
7. **DO NOT GET TRAPPED BY EVIL**
   - ☐ Proverbs 4:20-27
8. **DO NOT BE OVERCOME BY EVIL**
   - ☐ Romans 12:21
9. **DO NOT BE DECEIVED REGARDING EVIL**
   - ☐ 1 Corinthians 15:33
10. **DO NOT IMITATE WHAT IS EVIL**
    - ☐ 3 John 1:11

NOTES

Three prayers against evil
2 Corinthians 13:7

1. **KEEP ME FROM EVIL**
   ☐ 1 Chronicles 4:10

2. **DELIVER US FROM EVIL**
   ☐ Matthew 6:13

3. **KEEP US FROM THE EVIL ONE**
   ☐ John 17:15

SEPTEMBER 12
See To It (NIV)

1. **YOU ARE NOT ALARMED**
   ☐ Matthew 24:6

2. **YOU ARE NOT IN THE DARK**
   ☐ Luke 11:35

3. **YOU ARE NOT TAKEN CAPTIVE**
   ☐ Colossians 2:8

4. **YOU COMPLETE YOUR CALLING**
   ☐ Colossians 4:17

5. **YOU DO NOT HAVE A SINFUL, UNBELIEVING HEART**
   ☐ Hebrews 3:12

6. **YOU DON'T MISS THE GRACE OF GOD**
   ☐ Hebrews 12:15

7. **YOU DO NOT REFUSE TO LISTEN**
   ☐ Hebrews 12:25

SEPTEMBER 13

God Of *Matthew 22:32 (NIV)*

1. **ALL COMFORT**
   - ☐ 2 Corinthians 1:3

2. **ALL GRACE**
   - ☐ 1 Peter 5:10

3. **LOVE**
   - ☐ 2 Corinthians 13:11

4. **PEACE**
   - ☐ 1 Corinthians 14:33
   - ☐ Romans 15:33
   - ☐ Romans 16:20
   - ☐ Philippians 4:9
   - ☐ 1 Thessalonians 5:23
   - ☐ Hebrews 13:20

5. **HOPE**
   - ☐ Romans 15:13

6. **POWER AND STRENGTH**
   - ☐ Psalm 68:35

7. **JUSTICE**
   - ☐ Isaiah 30:18

SEPTEMBER 14

When You Face the Uncertainty of Difficulty: [Part 1] (NKJV)

1. **DO NOT WORRY OR FEAR**
   - ☐ Matthew 6:25-34
   - ☐ Exodus 14:13
   - ☐ Deuteronomy 31:8
   - ☐ Psalm 27:1
   - ☐ Isaiah 41:10
   - ☐ 2 Timothy 1:7

2. **SEEK FIRST THE KINGDOM OF GOD**
   - ☐ Matthew 6:33

3. **PRAY WITHOUT CEASING AND BE ANXIOUS FOR NOTHING**
   - ☐ 1 Thessalonians 5:17
   - ☐ Philippians 4:6
   - ☐ 1 Peter 5:7
   - ☐ Psalm 34:17

4. **LET THE PEACE OF CHRIST RULE IN YOUR HEART**
   - ☐ Colossians 3:15

5. **PUT ON THE WHOLE ARMOR OF GOD**
   - ☐ Ephesians 6:10-20

SEPTEMBER 15
When You Face the Uncertainty of Difficulty: [Part 2] (NKJV)

1. **GIVE THANKS IN ALL CIRCUMSTANCES**
   - ☐ 1 Thessalonians 5:18
   - ☐ Colossians 3:15

2. **TRUST IN THE LORD WITH ALL YOUR HEART**
   - ☐ Proverbs 3:5-6
   - ☐ Isaiah 26:3

3. **WALK BY FAITH AND NOT BY SIGHT**
   - ☐ 2 Corinthians 5:7
   - ☐ Matthew 21:22
   - ☐ Matthew 7:7-8

4. **KEEP YOUR EYES ON**
   - ☐ Christ
     - ☐ Hebrews 12:2
   - ☐ Things above
     - ☐ Colossians 3:2
   - ☐ The big picture of eternity
     - ☐ 2 Corinthians 4:16-18

5. RUN WITH ENDURANCE
- ☐ Hebrews 12:1

6. STAND ON GOD'S PROMISES
- ☐ Romans 4:21
- ☐ Romans 15:4
- ☐ 2 Corinthians 7:1

7. ABIDE IN CHRIST AND HIS PRESENCE
- ☐ John 15:4-10

SEPTEMBER 16

10 Keys to the Kingdom of Heaven in Matthew *Matthew 16:19 (NKJV)*

1. REPENTANCE
- ☐ Matthew 3:2
- ☐ Matthew 4:17

2. HUMILITY (POOR IN SPIRIT)
- ☐ Matthew 5:3

3. FAITHFULNESS (ENDURE PERSECUTION)
- ☐ Matthew 5:10

4. KEEPING THE COMMANDMENTS
- ☐ Matthew 5:19

5. RIGHTEOUSNESS THAT IS REAL
- ☐ Matthew 5:20

6. DOING THE WILL OF THE FATHER
- ☐ Matthew 7:21

7. EXERCISING OUR FAITH
- ☐ Matthew 8:10-11

8. **OPEN EYES AND EARS TO UNDERSTANDING**
   - ☐ Matthew 13:11-15

9. **SOLD OUT**
   - ☐ Matthew 13:44

10. **BECOMING LIKE LITTLE CHILDREN**
    - ☐ Matthew 18:1-4

SEPTEMBER 17
Seven Marks of a Disciple (NKJV)

1. **ABIDES IN HIS WORD**
   - ☐ John 8:31-32
   - ☐ John 15:7
   - ☐ 1 John 2:14

2. **SHARES A LOVE FOR ONE ANOTHER**
   - ☐ John 13:34-35
   - ☐ 1 John 4:20

3. **BEARS MUCH FRUIT**
   - ☐ John 15:8
   - ☐ The five levels of fruit
     - ☐ No fruit (John 15:2)
     - ☐ Fruit (John 15:2b)
     - ☐ Fruit that remains (John 15:16)
     - ☐ More fruit (John 15:2c)
     - ☐ Much fruit (John 15:5,8)

4. **ALLOWS CHRIST TO OCCUPY FIRST PLACE**
   - ☐ Luke 14:26
   - ☐ Luke 9:57-62

5. **TAKES UP THEIR CROSS AND FOLLOWS**
   - ☐ Luke 14:27
   - ☐ Luke 9:23

NOTES

6. **WILLING TO FORSAKE EVERYTHING**
   - ☐ Luke 14:33
   - ☐ Matthew 4:19-20
   - ☐ Matthew 19:27-29

7. **DESIRES TO BE LIKE THEIR TEACHER**
   - ☐ Matthew 10:24-25

SEPTEMBER 18
Beginning of Life Scriptures (NKJV)

- ☐ Genesis 1:27
- ☐ Genesis 9:5-6
- ☐ Exodus 20:13
- ☐ Exodus 21:22-25
- ☐ Exodus 23:7
- ☐ Deuteronomy 30:19
- ☐ *Job 33:4*
- ☐ *Job 10:11-12*
- ☐ Job 31:15
- ☐ Psalm 22:10-11
- ☐ Psalm 82:3
- ☐ *Psalm 100:3*
- ☐ *Psalm 119:73a*
- ☐ Psalm 127:3-5
- ☐ *Psalm 139:13-16*
- ☐ Proverbs 31:8
- ☐ Proverbs 24:11-12
- ☐ *Isaiah 44:24*
- ☐ Isaiah 49:1,5
- ☐ *Isaiah 64:8*
- ☐ Jeremiah 1:5
- ☐ *Matthew 1:20*
- ☐ *Luke 1:15,41-44*
- ☐ Galatians 1:15

SEPTEMBER 19
Seven Truths About Temptation
James 1:12-16 (NKJV)

1. **TEMPTATION IS NOT SIN**
   - ☐ James 1:12

2. **TEMPTATION IS SOMETHING WE MUST ALL FACE**
   - ☐ James 1:13

3. **TEMPTATION DOES NOT COME FROM GOD**
   - ☐ James 1:13

4. **TEMPTATION IS PERSONAL**
   - ☐ James 1:14

5. **TEMPTATION IS ENTICING**
   - ☐ James 1:14

6. **TEMPTATION IS DECEIVING**
   - ☐ James 1:16

7. **TEMPTATION CAN BE ENDURED AND OVERCOME**
   - ☐ James 1:12

SEPTEMBER 20
How to Overcome Temptation (NKJV)

1. **ON GUARD**
   - ☐ 1 Peter 5:8
   - ☐ Matthew 26:41
   - ☐ 1 Corinthians 10:12

2. **VIEW THE END RESULT**
   - ☐ Hebrews 11:24-25
   - ☐ James 1:15

3. **ESCAPE (LOOK FOR THE EXIT DOOR)**
   - ☐ 1 Corinthians 10:13
   - ☐ Genesis 39

4. **RESIST THE DEVIL**
   - ☐ James 4:7-8
   - ☐ 1 Peter 5:9

5. **CALL ON THE LORD FOR HELP**
   - ☐ Hebrews 2:18
   - ☐ Hebrews 4:15
   - ☐ 2 Peter 2:9

6. **ONGOING PRAYER AND FASTING**
   - ☐ Matthew 4:1-11
   - ☐ Matthew 6:13
   - ☐ Matthew 26:41
   - ☐ Luke 22:31-32,39-46

7. **MEDITATE ON GOD'S WORD DAILY**
   - ☐ Psalm 119:11
   - ☐ Matthew 4:4-9

8. **EXERCISE YOURSELF TO GODLINESS**
   - ☐ 1 Timothy 4:7
   - ☐ James 1:2-3

SEPTEMBER 21

Six Things We Can Learn About Prayer from the Garden

Mark 14:32-42 (NKJV)

1. **HE RECRUITED OTHERS TO PRAY WITH HIM**
   - ☐ Mark 14:32

2. **HE MADE HIS REQUESTS KNOWN TO GOD**
   - ☐ Mark 14:35
   - ☐ Philippians 4:6-7

3. **HE REPEATED HIS REQUESTS**
   - ☐ Mark 14:35
   - ☐ Mark 14:39
   - ☐ Mark 14:41

4. **HE RELIED ON THE HOLY SPIRIT**
   - ☐ Mark 14:38
   - ☐ Romans 8:27

5. **HE ALIGNED HIS PRAYER TO THE WILL OF THE FATHER**
   - ☐ Mark 14:36

6. **HE ACCEPTED AND ACTED ON THE WILL OF GOD**
   - ☐ Mark 14:42

SEPTEMBER 22
The Biblical Basis for Reaching the Lost (NKJV)

1. **JESUS CAME TO SEEK AND SAVE THE LOST**
   - ☐ Luke 19:10

2. **JESUS SENT OUT HIS DISCIPLES TO REACH THE LOST**
   - ☐ Matthew 10:6

3. **THE HARVEST FIELDS ARE RIPE**
   - ☐ John 4:35

4. **GOD IS NOT WILLING THAT ANY SHOULD PERISH**
   - ☐ 2 Peter 3:9

5. **UNLESS WE TELL THEM, HOW WILL THEY KNOW**
   - ☐ Romans 10:14

6. **HELL IS REAL**
   ☐ Luke 16:19-31

7. **TIME IS SHORT**
   ☐ Ephesians 5:15-16

SEPTEMBER 23
Jesus' Approach to Lost People (NIV)

1. **HE STAYED FOCUSED ON HIS MISSION TO SINNERS**
   ☐ Luke 4:42-43

2. **HE LOVED SINNERS**
   ☐ Romans 5:8

3. **HE SPENT TIME WITH SINNERS**
   ☐ Luke 5:30-32

4. **HE TALKED TO SINNERS**
   ☐ John 4:1-42

5. **HE BUILT FRIENDSHIP WITH SINNERS**
   ☐ Luke 7:32-34

6. **HE WELCOMED SINNERS**
   ☐ Luke 15:2

7. **HE FORGAVE SINNERS**
   ☐ John 8:1-11

SEPTEMBER 24
God Loves Us Even When (NKJV)

1. **WE SIN**
   - ☐ Romans 5:8
   - ☐ Psalm 86:15
   - ☐ Ephesians 2:4-5

2. **WE COME UNDER DIVINE DISCIPLINE**
   - ☐ Hebrews 12:6
   - ☐ Proverbs 3:11-12

3. **WE FALL SHORT**
   - ☐ Mark 10:21 (ESV)

4. **WE FAIL**
   - ☐ Matthew 26:31-35
   - ☐ Mark 14:27-31
   - ☐ Luke 22:31-34
   - ☐ John 13:31-38
   - ☐ John 21:15-25

5. **WE FEEL LET DOWN OR ABANDONED**
   - ☐ John 11:5-7

6. **WE FACE TRIALS AND HARDSHIPS**
   - ☐ Romans 8:35-39

7. **WE FACE DISAPPOINTMENT**
   - ☐ Romans 5:3-5

NOTES

SEPTEMBER 25

The Maze of God's Ways
Psalm 128:1 (NKJV)

1. **GOD'S WAYS ARE NOT OUR WAYS**
   - ☐ Isaiah 55:8
   - ☐ Proverbs 14:12
   - ☐ Proverbs 16:2,25
   - ☐ Proverbs 21:2

2. **GOD'S WAYS ARE RIGHT**
   - ☐ Hosea 14:9
   - ☐ Psalm 18:30
   - ☐ Revelation 15:3

3. **GOD'S WAYS ARE HIGHER THAN OUR WAYS**
   - ☐ Isaiah 55:9
   - ☐ Psalm 40:5
   - ☐ Psalm 139:1-18

4. **GOD'S WAYS ARE HOLY**
   - ☐ Psalm 77:13 (NLT)
   - ☐ Psalm 145:17

5. **GOD'S WAYS CAN BE KNOWN**
   - ☐ Ephesians 1:9
   - ☐ Psalm 103:7
   - ☐ Exodus 33:13

6. **GOD'S WAYS MUST BE SOUGHT**
   - ☐ Psalm 27:11
   - ☐ Psalm 86:11
   - ☐ Isaiah 2:3
   - ☐ Isaiah 58:2

7. **GOD'S WAYS ARE TO BE OBEYED**
   - ☐ Psalm 18:21
   - ☐ Psalm 128:1
   - ☐ Deuteronomy 5:33
   - ☐ Deuteronomy 8:6
   - ☐ Deuteronomy 10:12

8. GOD'S WAYS ARE TO BE MADE KNOWN
- ☐ Psalm 67:2

9. GOD'S WAYS ARE EVERLASTING
- ☐ Habakkuk 3:6
- ☐ Hebrews 13:8

SEPTEMBER 26
Hidden Sins *Proverbs 20:27 (NLT)*

1. GOD SEES AND KNOWS ABOUT WHAT WE THINK IS HIDDEN
- ☐ Isaiah 29:15
- ☐ Psalm 44:20-21
- ☐ Psalm 69:5
- ☐ Psalm 90:8
- ☐ Proverbs 15:11
- ☐ Job 34:22
- ☐ Jeremiah 16:17-18
- ☐ Jeremiah 23:24
- ☐ Hebrews 4:13

2. GOD WILL EVENTUALLY EXPOSE THE SIN WE HAVE HIDDEN IN OUR HEARTS
- ☐ Numbers 32:23
- ☐ Mark 4:22-23
- ☐ Luke 8:17
- ☐ Matthew 10:26

3. GOD WILL JUDGE US FOR OUR UNCONFESSED HIDDEN SINS
- ☐ Romans 2:16
- ☐ Ecclesiastes 12:14

4. GOD WILL FORGIVE OUR HIDDEN SINS IF WE CONFESS THEM
- ☐ 1 John 1:9
- ☐ Proverbs 28:13
- ☐ Psalm 32:3-5
- ☐ Psalm 19:12-13

NOTES

SEPTEMBER 27

Four Truths About Our Words
Proverbs 16:24 (NLT)

1. **OUR WORDS FLOW FROM THE HEART**
   - ☐ Luke 6:43-46
   - ☐ Matthew 12:34
   - ☐ Proverbs 4:23

2. **UNKIND WORDS ARE HARMFUL**
   - ☐ Proverbs 12:18
   - ☐ Proverbs 11:9
   - ☐ Proverbs 15:4
   - ☐ Proverbs 18:21
   - ☐ James 3:5-8

3. **KIND WORDS BRING HEALING**
   - ☐ Proverbs 12:18
   - ☐ Proverbs 12:25
   - ☐ Proverbs 15:1-4

4. **KIND WORDS HONOR GOD AND ARE PLEASING TO HIM**
   - ☐ Proverbs 15:26
   - ☐ Psalm 19:14
   - ☐ Colossians 3:17

SEPTEMBER 28

11 Things the Bible Tells You to Do With All Your Heart (NKJV)

1. **SEARCH FOR HIM WITH ALL YOUR HEART**
   - ☐ Deuteronomy 4:29

2. **SERVE HIM WITH ALL YOUR HEART**
   - ☐ Deuteronomy 10:12

3. **LOVE HIM WITH ALL YOUR HEART**
   ☐ Matthew 22:37

4. **OBEY HIM WITH ALL YOUR HEART**
   ☐ Deuteronomy 30:2-3

5. **TURN TO HIM WITH ALL YOUR HEART**
   ☐ Deuteronomy 30:10

6. **WORSHIP HIM WITH ALL YOUR HEART**
   ☐ Ephesians 5:19

7. **TRUST IN HIM WITH ALL YOUR HEART**
   ☐ Proverbs 3:5-6

8. **REJOICE WITH ALL YOUR HEART**
   ☐ Zephaniah 3:14

9. **RETURN TO THE LORD WITH ALL YOUR HEART**
   ☐ Joel 2:12

10. **WORK WITH ALL YOUR HEART**
    ☐ Colossians 3:23

11. **DO THE WILL OF GOD WITH ALL YOUR HEART**
    ☐ Ephesians 6:6

SEPTEMBER 29
The Daily Disciplines of a Disciple of Christ *1 Timothy 4:6-10 (NKJV)*

1. **READ AND STUDY THE SCRIPTURES**
   ☐ Acts 17:11
   ☐ Nehemiah 8:18
   ☐ Joshua 1:8
   ☐ Psalm 1:1-2

2. **PRAYER AND PRAISE**
   ☐ Psalm 88:9
   ☐ Psalm 96:1-3

3. **WAITING AND LISTENING**
   ☐ Proverbs 8:34

4. **WITNESS**
   ☐ Acts 17:17
   ☐ 1 Thessalonians 4:11-12 (NIV)

5. **ENCOURAGE ONE ANOTHER**
   ☐ Hebrews 3:13 (NIV)
   ☐ 1 Thessalonians 5:11 (NIV)

6. **SELF-DENIAL**
   ☐ Luke 9:23

7. **SURRENDER**
   ☐ 1 Corinthians 15:31

8. **FAITH INTO ACTION**
   ☐ James 2:14-15

SEPTEMBER 30
Prudent Behavior *Proverbs 1:3 (NIV)*

1. **OVERLOOKS AN INSULT**
   ☐ Proverbs 12:16

2. **HOLDS TONGUE**
   ☐ Proverbs 10:19
   ☐ Amos 5:13

3. **KEEPS MATTERS TO THEMSELVES**
   ☐ Proverbs 12:23

4. **ACTS OUT OF KNOWLEDGE**
   ☐ Proverbs 13:16

5. **GIVES THOUGHT TO THEIR STEPS**
   ☐ Proverbs 14:8,15

6. **SEES DANGER AND TAKES REFUGE**
   ☐ Proverbs 22:3
   ☐ Proverbs 27:12

OCTOBER

OCTOBER 1
Five Crowns in Scripture [NKJV]

1. **THE IMPERISHABLE CROWN**
   - ☐ 1 Corinthians 9:24-27
   - ☐ 1 Peter 1:3-5

2. **THE CROWN OF REJOICING**
   - ☐ 1 Thessalonians 2:17-20
   - ☐ Philippians 4:4

3. **THE CROWN OF RIGHTEOUSNESS**
   - ☐ 2 Timothy 4:6-8

4. **THE CROWN OF GLORY**
   - ☐ 1 Peter 5:1-4

5. **THE CROWN OF LIFE**
   - ☐ James 1:12
   - ☐ Revelation 2:9-11

OCTOBER 2
Six Different Types of Rewards [NKJV]

1. **NO REWARDS**
   - ☐ Matthew 5:43-48
   - ☐ Matthew 6:1

2. **FUTILE REWARDS**
   - ☐ Job 15:17-35

3. **IMMEDIATE REWARDS**
   - ☐ Matthew 6:2-5,16

4. **GREAT REWARDS**
   - ☐ Genesis 15:1
   - ☐ Ruth 2:11-22
   - ☐ Psalm 19:7-11
   - ☐ Matthew 5:11-12
   - ☐ Hebrews 10:35-36

5. LOST REWARDS
- [ ] 2 John 1:4-11

6. ETERNAL REWARDS
- [ ] Matthew 10:40-42
- [ ] 1 Corinthians 3:9-15
- [ ] Hebrews 11:24-28

OCTOBER 3
There Are Great Rewards in Heaven (NKJV)

1. FOR THOSE WHO LOVE THEIR ENEMIES
- [ ] Matthew 5:43-48
- [ ] Luke 6:35-36

2. FOR THOSE WHO SEEK HIM
- [ ] Matthew 6:5-6
- [ ] Hebrews 11:5-6

3. FOR THOSE WHO ARE GENUINE IN THEIR FAITH
- [ ] Matthew 6:1-2,4-6,16-20
- [ ] Matthew 19:16-30

4. FOR THOSE WHO HELP THE NEEDY
- [ ] Matthew 10:41-42
- [ ] Matthew 25:31-46
- [ ] Mark 9:41

5. FOR THOSE WHO SUFFER PERSECUTION
- [ ] Luke 6:22-23

NOTES

6. FOR THOSE WHO HAVE DONE GOOD DEEDS
- ☐ Matthew 16:24-27
- ☐ Psalm 62:11-12
- ☐ Jeremiah 17:9-10
- ☐ Jeremiah 32:17-20
- ☐ Ephesians 6:8

7. FOR THOSE WHO ARE RIGHTEOUS
- ☐ 2 Samuel 22:21
- ☐ Psalm 18:20
- ☐ Psalm 58:10-11
- ☐ Proverbs 11:18
- ☐ Matthew 10:40-42

OCTOBER 4
Three Regular Exams We Must Take
1 Corinthians 11:23-34 (NLT)

1. THE EXAMINATION OF OTHERS
- ☐ 1 Corinthians 9:3 (NASB)
- ☐ Proverbs 18:17 (NASB)
- ☐ Daniel 1:13-20 (NASB)
- ☐ Acts 4:9 (ESV)

2. THE EXAMINATION OF GOD
- ☐ 1 Chronicles 29:10-20
- ☐ Psalm 139:1
- ☐ Psalm 17:3
- ☐ Jeremiah 17:9-10
- ☐ Jeremiah 20:12
- ☐ Proverbs 5:21
- ☐ 1 Thessalonians 2:1-8 (NASB)

3. SELF-EXAMINATION
- ☐ 1 Corinthians 11:27-29
- ☐ 2 Corinthians 13:5-10
- ☐ Galatians 6:1-5 (NASB)
- ☐ Lamentations 3:40

OCTOBER 5

The 15 Attributes of the Pharisees:
[Part 1] (NKJV)

1. **THEY LACK GENUINE FRUIT**
   - ☐ Matthew 3:7-10

2. **THEY LIKE TO POINT OUT THE FAULTS OF OTHERS**
   - ☐ Matthew 12:1-8
   - ☐ John 8:1-11

3. **THEY DO NOT LIKE SINNERS**
   - ☐ Matthew 9:10-13
   - ☐ Luke 7:36-39

4. **THEY PLOT AGAINST OTHERS**
   - ☐ Matthew 12:1-14
   - ☐ Matthew 22:1-22

5. **THEY ARE CONFINED TO TRADITION**
   - ☐ Matthew 15:1-14
   - ☐ Mark 7:4-9

6. **THEY ARE ALWAYS TESTING AND TRICKING**
   - ☐ Matthew 19:3
   - ☐ Matthew 16:1
   - ☐ Matthew 22:35

7. **THEY ARE FOCUSED ON THE OPINION OF OTHERS** (crowd)
   - ☐ Matthew 21:45-46

NOTES

OCTOBER 6

The 15 Attributes of the Pharisees:
[Part 2] (NKJV)

8. **THEY DO NOT PRACTICE WHAT THEY PREACH**
   - ☐ Matthew 23:3

9. **THEY PUT HEAVY LOADS ON OTHERS**
   - ☐ Matthew 23:4

10. **THEY FOCUS MORE ON OUTWARD APPEARANCE**
    - ☐ Matthew 23:5,25-28

11. **THEY LOVE THE PLACES OF HONOR**
    - ☐ Matthew 23:6

12. **THEY NEGLECT THE KEY PARTS OF THE LAW**
    - ☐ Matthew 23:23

13. **THEY REJECT GOD'S PURPOSE**
    - ☐ Luke 7:30

14. **THEY SEE THEMSELVES AS BETTER THAN OTHERS**
    - ☐ Luke 18:9-14

15. **THEY ARE FILLED WITH JEALOUSY**
    - ☐ John 4:1

OCTOBER 7

Six Things Jesus Did to Accomplish the Will of God *Colossians 1:1-14 (NLT)*

1. **HE SOUGHT GOD AND HIS WILL THROUGH PRAYER**
   - ☐ Matthew 6:9-10
   - ☐ 1 John 5:14-15
   - ☐ Matthew 26:39-44

2. **HE PURPOSED IN HIS HEART TO DO THE WILL OF GOD**
   - [ ] John 6:38
   - [ ] Acts 21:12-14
   - [ ] Hebrews 10:5-10
   - [ ] Ephesians 6:6

3. **HE FOUND NOURISHMENT FROM DOING GOD'S WILL**
   - [ ] John 4:34
   - [ ] Matthew 7:21
   - [ ] Psalm 40:8
   - [ ] 1 Peter 4:1-2
   - [ ] John 9:31

4. **HE WILLINGLY SURRENDERED HIS OWN WILL IN EXCHANGE FOR GOD'S WILL**
   - [ ] Luke 22:42
   - [ ] John 5:30

5. **HE ALIGNED HIS WILL TO THE WORD OF GOD**
   - [ ] Psalm 119:105
   - [ ] John 7:17

6. **HE CARRIED OUT HIS FATHER'S WILL TO COMPLETION**
   - [ ] John 4:34
   - [ ] John 5:36
   - [ ] John 17:4
   - [ ] John 19:30
   - [ ] Hebrews 12:2
   - [ ] Acts 13:22

BEFORE YOU PUT THE SHOVEL DOWN
- [ ] Proverbs 3:5-6
- [ ] Psalm 143:10
- [ ] Hebrews 13:20-21

NOTES

OCTOBER 8
Six Present Things God Rescues Us From (NLT)

1. **DOMINION OF DARKNESS**
   ☐ Colossians 1:11-14

2. **EVERY EVIL ATTACK**
   ☐ 2 Timothy 4:16-18

3. **TRIALS**
   ☐ 2 Peter 2:9

4. **PERSECUTION**
   ☐ 2 Timothy 3:10-13 (NIV)

5. **DESPAIR**
   ☐ 2 Corinthians 1:8-11 (MSG)

6. **TROUBLES**
   ☐ Acts 7:9-10

OCTOBER 9
Four Keys to "Whatever We Ask" in Prayer (NKJV)

1. **IN HIS NAME**
   ☐ John 14:12-14
   ☐ John 15:16
   ☐ John 16:23-24

2. **ACCORDING TO HIS WILL**
   ☐ 1 John 5:14-15
   ☐ Matthew 26:39
   ☐ 2 Corinthians 12:7-10

3. **BELIEVING**
   - [ ] Matthew 21:21-22
   - [ ] James 1:5-6

4. **IN OBEDIENCE**
   - [ ] 1 John 3:21-22

OCTOBER 10
Four Contaminating Spirits Within a Congregation *Exodus 2:23-25, Numbers 14:30 (NLT)*

1. **A COMPLAINING SPIRIT**
   - [ ] Exodus 15-17
   - [ ] Numbers 11:1-6
   - [ ] Numbers 14:2,27-29
   - [ ] Acts 6:1
   - [ ] Philippians 2:14-16

2. **A CRITICAL SPIRIT**
   - [ ] Numbers 12:1-8
   - [ ] Mark 14:3-9
   - [ ] Acts 11:1-4
   - [ ] James 4:1-3
   - [ ] Romans 14:10-13

3. **A COWARDLY SPIRIT**
   - [ ] Numbers 13:32
   - [ ] Numbers 14:36
   - [ ] Revelation 21:8

4. **A SPIRIT OF CONTEMPT**
   - [ ] Numbers 14:11
   - [ ] Numbers 14:23-44
   - [ ] Numbers 15:31

Notice the different spirits in the congregation:

1. **SPIRIT OF MOSES IS A SPIRIT OF HUMILITY**
   - [ ] Numbers 11:16,25;12:3

2. **SPIRIT OF JOSHUA IS A SPIRIT OF STRENGTH AND COURAGE**
   ☐ Joshua 1

3. **SPIRIT OF CALEB IS A SPIRIT OF WHOLEHEARTED LOYALTY**
   ☐ Numbers 14:24 (NIV)

OCTOBER 11

Some Facts About God's Love
1 John 4:8 (NKJV)

1. **GOD'S LOVE IS SACRIFICIAL AND DISPLAYED THROUGH HIS SON**
   ☐ John 3:16-17

2. **GOD'S LOVE IS GREAT FOR US**
   ☐ Ephesians 2:4-5
   ☐ John 17:23

3. **GOD DEMONSTRATES HIS LOVE TO US EVEN WHILE WE WERE SINNERS**
   ☐ Romans 5:8

4. **GOD'S LOVE IS POURED OUT THROUGH THE HOLY SPIRIT IN OUR HEARTS**
   ☐ Romans 5:5

5. **NOTHING CAN SEPARATE US FROM HIS LOVE**
   ☐ Romans 8:38-39

6. **GOD'S LOVE IS TO BE EXPRESSED TO OTHERS**
   ☐ John 13:34-35
   ☐ 1 John 4:11-12

7. **GOD'S LOVE ENDURES FOREVER**
   - ☐ Psalm 136:26
   - ☐ Jeremiah 31:3

8. **GOD'S LOVE INVOLVES DISCIPLINE**
   - ☐ Hebrews 12:5-6

9. **GOD'S LOVE IS PROVEN IN OUR ACTIONS TOWARD OTHERS**
   - ☐ 1 John 3:16-17

10. **GOD INITIATES HIS LOVE TOWARD US**
    - ☐ 1 John 4:10,19

OCTOBER 12
Don't Be Surprised (NLT)

1. **YOU MUST BE BORN AGAIN**
   - ☐ John 3:7

2. **YOU ARE GOING THROUGH TRIALS**
   - ☐ 1 Peter 4:12-13
   - ☐ 2 Timothy 3:12
   - ☐ 1 Peter 1:6-7
   - ☐ 1 Thessalonians 3:2-4

3. **YOU ARE HATED BY THE WORLD**
   - ☐ 1 John 3:11-13
   - ☐ John 15:18-19
   - ☐ John 17:14
   - ☐ Luke 21:17

4. **YOU WILL SEE THE LORD'S RETURN AS A THIEF IN THE NIGHT**
   - ☐ 1 Thessalonians 5:1-11

OCTOBER 13

What the Bible Says About Self-control (NLT)

1. **IT IS A FRUIT OF THE SPIRIT**
   ☐ Galatians 5:22-23

2. **A LACK OF IT CAN BE DEADLY**
   ☐ Proverbs 5:23

3. **IT IS BETTER TO POSSESS THAN THE ABILITY TO CONQUER**
   ☐ Proverbs 16:32

4. **YOU ARE DEFENSELESS WITHOUT IT**
   ☐ Proverbs 25:28

5. **A LACK OF IT IS AN OPPORTUNITY FOR SATAN TO ATTACK**
   ☐ 1 Corinthians 7:1-5

6. **WE ARE TO EXERCISE SELF-CONTROL**
   ☐ 1 Peter 1:13
   ☐ 1 Timothy 3:2
   ☐ Titus 2:1-2

7. **IN THE LAST DAYS THERE WILL BE AN INCREASE OF THE SHORTAGE OF IT**
   ☐ 2 Timothy 3:1-5

8. **WE SHOULD PRAY FOR SELF-CONTROL**
   ☐ 1 Peter 4:7 (ESV)

9. **WE ARE TO STAY AWAY FROM THOSE WHO LACK SELF-CONTROL**
   ☐ 2 Timothy 3:3-5

10. **IT IS NECESSARY TO LIVE A GODLY LIFE**
    ☐ 2 Peter 1:3-11

OCTOBER 14
Stay Away From [NLT]

1. **ANYTHING THAT IS IMPURE**
   - ☐ Deuteronomy 23:9

2. **EVERY EVIL**
   - ☐ Psalm 101:4
   - ☐ 1 Thessalonians 5:22

3. **CORRUPT SPEECH**
   - ☐ Proverbs 4:24

4. **THE TEMPTATION OF SEXUAL SIN**
   - ☐ Proverbs 5:8
   - ☐ 1 Thessalonians 4:3

5. **FOOLS**
   - ☐ Proverbs 14:7

6. **IDOLS**
   - ☐ Hosea 14:8

7. **BELIEVERS WHO LIVE IDOL LIVES**
   - ☐ 2 Thessalonians 3:6-7

8. **THOSE WHO REFUSE TO OBEY**
   - ☐ 2 Thessalonians 3:14-15

9. **THOSE WHO CAUSE DIVISIONS**
   - ☐ Romans 16:17

10. **THOSE WHO LACK SELF-CONTROL**
    - ☐ 2 Timothy 3:1-5

OCTOBER 15

The Only Two Things That Amazed Jesus (NLT)

1. **UNBELIEF**
   - ☐ Mark 6:5-6
   - ☐ Mark 9:24
   - ☐ Mark 16:14
   - ☐ John 12:37
   - ☐ Hebrews 3:19

2. **GREAT FAITH**
   - ☐ Matthew 8:5-10 (NKJV)
   - ☐ Matthew 15:28 (NKJV)

OCTOBER 16

Standing on the Promises (NKJV)

1. **THEY ARE AVAILABLE TO US FOR OUR ASSURANCE**
   - ☐ 2 Peter 1:3-4

2. **THEY ARE EXCEEDINGLY GREAT AND PRECIOUS**
   - ☐ 2 Peter 1:3-4

3. **THEY ARE OBTAINED THROUGH FAITH**
   - ☐ Hebrews 11:32-34
   - ☐ Romans 4:13-21

4. **THEY ARE PROVEN THROUGH PATIENCE**
   - ☐ Hebrews 6:11-15
   - ☐ Hebrews 10:36
   - ☐ Romans 15:1-4 (NLT)

5. THEY CAN BE COUNTED ON BECAUSE GOD CANNOT LIE
- ☐ Titus 1:1-3
- ☐ Numbers 23:19 (NIV)
- ☐ 2 Samuel 22:31 (NLT)

6. THEY ENCOURAGE US TO RESPOND
- ☐ 2 Corinthians 7:1
- ☐ 2 Peter 1:5 (NLT)

7. THEY ARE IN HIM— YES AND AMEN
- ☐ 2 Corinthians 1:20
- ☐ Romans 15:8
- ☐ Acts 13:23
- ☐ Luke 1:69-73

8. THEY WILL BE FAITHFULLY FULFILLED BY GOD
- ☐ Hebrews 10:23
- ☐ Hebrews 11:11
- ☐ Psalm 71:22 (NLT)
- ☐ Daniel 9:4 (NLT)
- ☐ Psalm 119:140 (NIV)

OCTOBER 17
You Can Be Sure (NLT)

1. YOUR SINS WILL FIND YOU OUT
- ☐ Numbers 32:23

2. GOD HEARS OUR CRY
- ☐ Exodus 6:5

3. GOD'S WORDS ARE TRUE
- ☐ 2 Kings 10:10

4. **THE LORD SET APART THE GODLY FOR HIMSELF**
   ☐ Psalm 4:3

5. **GOD WILL RESCUE HIS PEOPLE**
   ☐ Zechariah 8:7-8

6. **NO IMMORAL PERSON WILL ENTER THE KINGDOM OF HEAVEN**
   ☐ Ephesians 5:3-5

7. **WHOEVER RETURNS A SINNER WILL HAVE A GREAT IMPACT**
   ☐ James 5:19-20

OCTOBER 18

Five Things to Do Without Wavering
1 Kings 18:21 (NLT)

1. **MAINTAINING INNOCENCE**
   ☐ Job 27:6

2. **FOLLOWING GOD**
   ☐ Psalm 17:5

3. **TRUSTING GOD**
   ☐ Psalm 26:1

4. **OBEYING**
   ☐ 1 Timothy 6:11-14

5. **HOLDING TIGHTLY TO OUR HOPE IN GOD**
   ☐ Hebrews 10:23

BEFORE YOU PUT THE SHOVEL DOWN
   ☐ Romans 4:19-20

OCTOBER 19

The Lord is My [NLT]

1. **STRENGTH**
   - ☐ Exodus 15:2
   - ☐ Psalm 28:7
   - ☐ Psalm 118:14

2. **BANNER**
   - ☐ Exodus 17:15

3. **ROCK**
   - ☐ 2 Samuel 22:2-3
   - ☐ Psalm 18:2

4. **SHEPHERD**
   - ☐ Psalm 23:1

5. **LIGHT AND SALVATION**
   - ☐ Psalm 27:1

6. **FORTRESS**
   - ☐ Psalm 94:22

7. **INHERITANCE**
   - ☐ Lamentations 3:24

8. **HELPER**
   - ☐ Hebrews 13:6
   - ☐ Psalm 46:1

NOTES

OCTOBER 20

The Pledge *Psalm 101:1-8 (NLT)*

The phrase "I will" appears 11 times in eight verses.

I will:

1. **PRAISE GOD WITH A SONG IN MY HEART**
   - ☐ Psalm 101:1
   - ☐ Psalm 9:1
   - ☐ Psalm 18:49
   - ☐ Psalm 34:1

2. **BE CAREFUL TO LIVE A BLAMELESS LIFE**
   - ☐ Psalm 101:2a
   - ☐ 1 Thessalonians 5:23
   - ☐ Philippians 1:10

3. **LEAD A LIFE OF INTEGRITY**
   - ☐ Psalm 101:2b
   - ☐ Job 1:1,8
   - ☐ Job 2:3
   - ☐ Proverbs 10:9
   - ☐ Titus 2:7

4. **REFUSE TO LOOK AT ANYTHING VILE OR VULGAR**
   - ☐ Psalm 101:3a
   - ☐ Job 31:1
   - ☐ Proverbs 4:25
   - ☐ Psalm 119:37
   - ☐ Matthew 5:27-30

5. **HAVE NOTHING TO DO WITH CROOKEDNESS**
   - ☐ Psalm 101:3b
   - ☐ Proverbs 2:13-15
   - ☐ Philippians 2:15
   - ☐ Acts 2:40
   - ☐ Matthew 7:13-14

6. **REJECT PERVERSE IDEAS AND EVERY KIND OF EVIL**
   - ☐ Psalm 101:4
   - ☐ 1 Timothy 4:7
   - ☐ 1 Thessalonians 5:22

7. **NOT TOLERATE SLANDER, LYING, PRIDE OR DECEPTION**
   - ☐ Psalm 101:6-7
   - ☐ Revelation 2:14

8. **SEARCH FOR FAITHFUL COMPANIONS**
   - ☐ Psalm 101:6b

OCTOBER 21
Six Benchmarks of the Born Again (NKJV)

1. **PRACTICES RIGHTEOUSNESS**
   - ☐ 1 John 2:29
   - ☐ 1 John 3:7

2. **DOES NOT PRACTICE SIN**
   - ☐ 1 John 3:9
   - ☐ 1 John 5:18

3. **SHOWS LOVE FOR ONE ANOTHER**
   - ☐ 1 John 4:7-8

4. **BELIEVES THAT JESUS IS CHRIST**
   - ☐ 1 John 5:1

5. **LOVES THE FATHER**
   - ☐ 1 John 5:1

6. **OVERCOMES**
   - ☐ 1 John 5:4-5

NOTES

OCTOBER 22
Serve the Lord [NKJV]

1. **WITH FAITHFULNESS**
   - ☐ Joshua 24:14 (NIV)
   - ☐ 1 Samuel 12:24 (NIV)

2. **WITH FEAR**
   - ☐ Psalm 2:11
   - ☐ 1 Samuel 12:24

3. **WITH GLADNESS**
   - ☐ Psalm 100:2
   - ☐ Romans 12:11

4. **WITH ALL YOUR HEART**
   - ☐ 1 Samuel 12:20
   - ☐ Deuteronomy 10:12-13
   - ☐ Deuteronomy 11:13-15
   - ☐ Joshua 22:5

5. **WITHOUT DISTRACTION**
   - ☐ 1 Corinthians 7:35

6. **WITH GREAT HUMILITY**
   - ☐ Acts 20:19

OCTOBER 23
Beware of Greed *Luke 12:15 (NLT)*

1. **BECAUSE GREED IS A SIN**
   - ☐ Mark 7:21-22
   - ☐ Ephesians 5:3-5
   - ☐ 2 Peter 2:14
   - ☐ Colossians 3:5

2. **BECAUSE GREED IS NEVER SATISFIED**
   - ☐ Job 20:20
   - ☐ Proverbs 21:26
   - ☐ Ecclesiastes 5:10
   - ☐ Isaiah 56:11
   - ☐ Habakkuk 2:5

3. **BECAUSE GREED ROBS YOU OF YOUR LIFE**
   - ☐ Proverbs 1:19
   - ☐ Romans 1:29
   - ☐ Matthew 23:25
   - ☐ Jeremiah 22:17

4. **BECAUSE GREED CAUSES FIGHTS**
   - ☐ Proverbs 28:25

5. **BECAUSE GREED WILL BE PUNISHED**
   - ☐ Isaiah 57:17

6. **BECAUSE GREED IMPACTS RELATIONSHIPS**
   - ☐ 1 Corinthians 5:11
   - ☐ Proverbs 15:27

7. **BECAUSE THE GREEDY WILL NOT INHERIT THE KINGDOM OF GOD**
   - ☐ 1 Corinthians 6:10
   - ☐ Ephesians 5:5

OCTOBER 24
Paul's Six Charges to Timothy (NIV)

1. **NOT TO TEACH FALSE DOCTRINE**
   - ☐ 1 Timothy 1:3

2. **KEEP INSTRUCTIONS WITHOUT PARTIALITY**
   - ☐ 1 Timothy 5:21

3. **FIGHT THE GOOD FIGHT OF FAITH**
   - ☐ 1 Timothy 6:13
   - ☐ 1 Timothy 1:18 (ESV)

4. **NOT TO BE HAUGHTY OR SET YOUR HOPES IN UNCERTAIN RICHES**
   - ☐ 1 Timothy 6:17 (ESV)

5. **PREACH THE WORD**
   - ☐ 2 Timothy 4:1-2

6. **DO YOUR BEST TO PRESENT YOURSELF APPROVED UNTO GOD**
   - ☐ 2 Timothy 2:14-16 (ESV)

OCTOBER 25
What the Bible Teaches About Our Reputation Hebrews 11:2-39 (NLT)

1. **IT IS A REQUIREMENT OF LEADERSHIP**
   - ☐ Deuteronomy 1:13
   - ☐ 1 Chronicles 5:24
   - ☐ 1 Timothy 3:2

2. **A GOOD REPUTATION BRINGS HONOR TO THE LORD**
   - ☐ 1 Kings 10:1

3. **A GOOD REPUTATION WILL BE REWARDED**
   - ☐ Nehemiah 9:10

4. **KINDNESS AND TRUTH ARE ESSENTIAL TO A GOOD REPUTATION**
   - ☐ Proverbs 3:4

5. **A GOOD REPUTATION IS BETTER THAN RICHES**
   - ☐ Proverbs 22:1
   - ☐ Ecclesiastes 7:1

6. **IF YOU DAMAGE YOUR REPUTATION, IT IS HARD TO REGAIN**
   ☐ Proverbs 25:10

7. **YOU CAN HAVE A FALSE REPUTATION**
   ☐ Revelation 3:1

OCTOBER 26
The Riches of God *Ephesians 3:8 (NIV)*

1. **THE RICHES OF HIS GRACE**
   ☐ Ephesians 1:7
   ☐ Ephesians 2:7

2. **THE RICHES OF HIS MERCY**
   ☐ Ephesians 2:4

3. **THE RICHES OF HIS GLORY**
   ☐ Ephesians 1:18
   ☐ Ephesians 3:16
   ☐ Philippians 4:19
   ☐ Colossians 1:27

4. **THE RICHES OF HIS KINDNESS**
   ☐ Ephesians 2:7

5. **THE RICHES OF HIS GOODNESS**
   ☐ Romans 2:4 (NKJV)

6. **THE RICHES OF HIS WISDOM**
   ☐ Romans 11:33

7. **THE RICHES OF FAITH IN HIM**
   ☐ James 2:5

8. **THE RICHES OF HIS FULL ASSURANCE**
   ☐ Colossians 2:2 (NKJV)

NOTES

OCTOBER 27
If We Wait on the Lord (NKJV)

1. **WE WILL NOT BE ASHAMED**
   - ☐ Psalm 25:3-5
   - ☐ Isaiah 49:23

2. **WE WILL RENEW OUR STRENGTH**
   - ☐ Isaiah 40:31
   - ☐ Psalm 27:14

3. **WE WILL RECEIVE A BLESSING**
   - ☐ Isaiah 30:18
   - ☐ Daniel 12:12

4. **WE WILL INHERIT THE EARTH**
   - ☐ Psalm 37:9

5. **WE WILL BE DELIVERED**
   - ☐ Psalm 39:7
   - ☐ Proverbs 20:22

6. **WE WILL WITNESS HIS PROVISION**
   - ☐ Psalm 33:20

7. **WE WILL DISCOVER IT WAS WORTH IT**
   - ☐ Lamentations 3:25
   - ☐ Isaiah 64:4
   - ☐ Psalm 52:9
   - ☐ Habakkuk 2:3

8. **WE WILL BE OBEDIENT**
   - ☐ Psalm 27:14
   - ☐ Zephaniah 3:8

NOTES

OCTOBER 28
Waiting Commands [NKJV]

1. **WAIT PATIENTLY**
   - ☐ Psalm 37:7
   - ☐ Psalm 40:1
   - ☐ James 5:7

2. **WAIT SILENTLY**
   - ☐ Psalm 62:1-5

3. **WAIT EXTENDEDLY**
   - ☐ Psalm 25:5

4. **WAIT CONTINUALLY**
   - ☐ Hosea 12:6

5. **WAIT COURAGEOUSLY**
   - ☐ Psalm 27:14

6. **WAIT EXPECTANTLY**
   - ☐ Psalm 130:5-6

OCTOBER 29
Seven New Testament Secrets to Living in the Light [NKJV]

1. **FOLLOW CHRIST**
   - ☐ John 8:12

2. **LET THE WORD OF GOD GUIDE YOU**
   - ☐ 2 Peter 1:19-20
   - ☐ Psalm 119:105

3. **PUT ASIDE THE DEEDS OF DARKNESS**
   - ☐ Romans 13:12

4. **HAVE NOTHING TO DO WITH THE DEEDS OF DARKNESS**
   - ☐ Ephesians 5:11

5. **DO NOT BE UNEQUALLY YOKED**
   - [ ] 2 Corinthians 6:14

6. **WALK WHILE YOU HAVE THE LIGHT**
   - [ ] John 12:35
   - [ ] 1 John 1:7

7. **PUT ON THE FULL ARMOR OF GOD**
   - [ ] Ephesians 6:12-13

OCTOBER 30
An Abomination to the Lord
Luke 16:15 (NKJV)

- [ ] Proverbs 3:32
- [ ] Proverbs 6:16-19
- [ ] Proverbs 11:1,20
- [ ] Proverbs 12:22
- [ ] Proverbs 15:8-9,26
- [ ] Proverbs 16:5,12
- [ ] Proverbs 17:15
- [ ] Proverbs 20:10,23
- [ ] Proverbs 21:27
- [ ] Proverbs 28:9

OCTOBER 31
The Word on Witchcraft (NKJV)

- [ ] Exodus 22:18
- [ ] Leviticus 19:31
- [ ] Leviticus 20:6, 27
- [ ] 1 Samuel 15:23
- [ ] 1 Chronicles 10:13-14
- [ ] 2 Chronicles 33:6
- [ ] Isaiah 8:19
- [ ] Acts 19:19
- [ ] Galatians 5:19-21
- [ ] Revelation 21:8
- [ ] Revelation 22:15

NOVEMBER

NOVEMBER 1

The Four "Alls" in the Great Commission *Matthew 28:18-20 (NKJV)*

1. **ALL AUTHORITY**
   - ☐ Matthew 28:18

2. **ALL NATIONS**
   - ☐ Matthew 28:19

3. **ALL THINGS**
   - ☐ Matthew 28:20

4. **ALL THE DAYS**
   - ☐ Matthew 28:20b (AMP)

John Stott said, "His authority on earth allows us to dare go to all the nations. His authority in heaven gives us our only hope of success. And His presence with us leaves us no other choice."

NOVEMBER 2

Six Ways to Pray for the Missions Message *1 Thessalonians 5:25 (NIV)*

1. **PRAY FOR OPEN DOORS FOR THE MESSAGE**
   - ☐ Colossians 4:2-4
   - ☐ Matthew 7:7-8
   - ☐ Acts 14:27
   - ☐ 1 Corinthians 16:9

2. **PRAY FOR THE MESSAGE TO BE PROCLAIMED CLEARLY**
   - ☐ Colossians 4:4

3. **PRAY FOR THE MESSENGER TO BE FEARLESS**
   - ☐ Ephesians 6:19-20
   - ☐ Acts 9:27
   - ☐ Jeremiah 1:17-18

4. **PRAY FOR THE MESSAGE TO SPREAD RAPIDLY**
   - ☐ 2 Thessalonians 3:1
   - ☐ Acts 2:47
   - ☐ Acts 6:1
   - ☐ Acts 6:7
   - ☐ Acts 12:24
   - ☐ Acts 19:20
   - ☐ 2 Corinthians 2:14

5. **PRAY THAT EVERYONE MAY HEAR IT**
   - ☐ 2 Timothy 4:17
   - ☐ Romans 10:14-17

6. **PRAY FOR THE FINANCING OF THE MESSAGE**
   - ☐ Romans 15:23-32
   - ☐ Romans 10:14-17
   - ☐ Philippians 4:6-10

NOVEMBER 3
10 Duties of a Congregation to Their Pastor: [Part 1] (NKJV)

1. **PRAY FOR THEM**
   - ☐ 1 Timothy 2:1-2

2. **OBEY THEM**
   - ☐ Hebrews 13:17

3. **SUPPORT THEM**
   - ☐ 1 Timothy 5:17-18

4. **REMEMBER THEM**
   - ☐ Hebrews 13:7

5. **ENCOURAGE THEM**
   - ☐ Romans 1:12

NOVEMBER 4

10 Duties of a Congregation to Their Pastor: [Part 2] (NKJV)

1. **CARE FOR THEM**
   - ☐ Philippians 2:25

2. **LOVE THEM**
   - ☐ 1 Thessalonians 5:13
   - ☐ Philemon 7

3. **RESPECT THEM**
   - ☐ 1 Thessalonians 5:12

4. **HONOR THEM**
   - ☐ Acts 20:10

5. **HELP THEM**
   - ☐ 2 Corinthians 9:1-2
   - ☐ Ephesians 4:12

NOVEMBER 5

Six Things That Will Help Us Be Strong 1 Corinthians 16:13 (NIV)

1. **HUMAN WEAKNESS**
   - ☐ 1 Corinthians 1:27
   - ☐ 2 Corinthians 12:10
   - ☐ 2 Corinthians 13:9

2. **FAITH IN CHRIST**
   - ☐ Romans 1:11
   - ☐ Romans 15:1

3. **FULL ARMOR OF GOD**
   - ☐ Ephesians 6:10

4. **GRACE OF JESUS**
   - ☐ 2 Timothy 2:1-2
   - ☐ 1 Corinthians 1:8

5. **SUFFERING**
   - ☐ 1 Peter 5:10

6. **WORD OF GOD**
   - ☐ 1 John 2:14

NOVEMBER 6
Seven Things Scripture Teaches Us About Persecution: [Part 1] (NKJV)

Getting started:
- ☐ Matthew 10:16-20
- ☐ Matthew 22-23
- ☐ John 15:18-21 (NKJV)

1. **ALL WHO DESIRE TO LIVE GODLY IN CHRIST JESUS WILL SUFFER PERSECUTION**
   - ☐ 2 Timothy 3:12
   - ☐ John 15:20
   - ☐ John 16:33

2. **PERSECUTION WILL INCREASE AND INTENSIFY AS YOU SEE THE DAY OF THE LORD APPROACHING**
   - ☐ 2 Timothy 3:1
   - ☐ Luke 21:12

NOTES

3. **SPIRITUAL BENEFITS AND BLESSINGS COME FROM TIMES OF PERSECUTION**
   - ☐ Matthew 5:10-12
   - ☐ Philippians 1:29
   - ☐ 1 Peter 3:14

THE FOUR IMMEDIATE BENEFITS RESULTING FROM PERSECUTION [Acts 8, (NLT)]**:**
   - ☐ The followers of Christ were scattered throughout the world (*Acts 8:1, NLT*)
   - ☐ The word of God spread (*Acts 8:4, NLT*)
   - ☐ It solidified the true believers (*Acts 8:5, NLT*)
     a. Matthew 13:20-21
   - ☐ It brought a greater dependence and reliance upon the Spirit of God (*Acts 8:7ff, NLT*)
     m. 1 Peter 5:10

NOVEMBER 7
Seven Things Scripture Teaches Us About Persecution: [Part 2] (NKJV)

4. **WE CAN REJOICE WHEN WE GO THROUGH PERSECUTION ON EARTH BECAUSE OUR REWARD IS GREAT IN HEAVEN**
   - ☐ Matthew 5:11-12
   - ☐ Acts 5:41
   - ☐ 1 Peter 4:16
   - ☐ Romans 5:3
   - ☐ Acts 14:22
   - ☐ 2 Corinthians 7:4
   - ☐ Revelation 7:14
   - ☐ 2 Corinthians 12:10

5. **WE ARE TO ENDURE SEASONS OF TRIBULATION AND PERSECUTION**
   - ☐ 1 Corinthians 4:12
   - ☐ Revelation 2:8-10
   - ☐ 2 Thessalonians 1:4
   - ☐ 2 Timothy 3:10-11
   - ☐ James 5:10-11
   - ☐ Hebrews 12:3

6. **WHEN WE FACE PERSECUTION, WE HAVE NOT BEEN FORSAKEN**
   - ☐ 2 Corinthians 4:8-9
   - ☐ Romans 8:35
   - ☐ Hebrews 11:37-40
   - ☐ Acts 7:9

7. **WE ARE TO PRAY AND BLESS THOSE WHO PERSECUTE US**
   - ☐ Romans 12:14
   - ☐ Matthew 5:44
   - ☐ John 12:24-26

NOVEMBER 8
We Will Give an Account
Psalm 10:13-16 (NIV)

1. **OF OUR PAST**
   - ☐ Ecclesiastes 3:15

2. **OF EVERY CARELESS WORD**
   - ☐ Matthew 12:36

3. **OF OUR TALENTS**
   - ☐ Luke 16:2

4. **OF OURSELVES**
   - ☐ Romans 14:12

5. **OF OUR SECRETS**
   - ☐ Hebrews 4:13

6. **OF OUR LEADERSHIP**
   - ☐ Hebrews 13:17

7. **OF OUR RECKLESS LIVING**
   - ☐ 1 Peter 4:1-5

NOTES

NOVEMBER 9
Six Common Struggles (NIV)

1. **STRUGGLE AGAINST SIN**
   ☐ Hebrews 12:4

2. **STRUGGLE AGAINST THE POWERS OF DARKNESS**
   ☐ Ephesians 6:12

3. **STRUGGLE WITH GOD**
   ☐ Genesis 32:28
   ☐ Hosea 12:3-4

4. **STRUGGLE WITH SUFFERING**
   ☐ Philippians 1:29-30
   ☐ Hebrews 10:32 (NKJV)

5. **STRUGGLE TO FULFILL GOD'S PURPOSE**
   ☐ Colossians 1:29
   ☐ Colossians 2:1

6. **STRUGGLE IN PRAYER**
   ☐ Romans 15:30

NOVEMBER 10
Seven Keys to Justification
Acts 13:39 (NIV)

1. **JUSTIFIED BY GRACE**
   ☐ Titus 3:7

2. **JUSTIFIED BY HUMILITY**
   ☐ Luke 18:14

3. **JUSTIFIED BY BELIEVING**
   ☐ Acts 13:39

4. **JUSTIFIED THROUGH FAITH**
   - ☐ Romans 5:1
   - ☐ Romans 3:28

5. **JUSTIFIED BY HIS BLOOD**
   - ☐ Romans 5:9

6. **JUSTIFIED IN THE NAME OF JESUS**
   - ☐ 1 Corinthians 6:11

7. **JUSTIFIED BY WORKS**
   - ☐ James 2:24 (NKJV)

NOVEMBER 11
Three Degrees of Trusting God
Jeremiah 17:5-7 (NLT)

There are those who:

1. **DO NOT TRUST GOD AND PUT THEIR TRUST IN OTHER THINGS**
   - ☐ Deuteronomy 1:32-33
   - ☐ Deuteronomy 9:23
   - ☐ 2 Chronicles 16:7
   - ☐ Psalm 52:7
   - ☐ Psalm 78:22,32
   - ☐ Psalm 118:8-9
   - ☐ Proverbs 11:28
   - ☐ Isaiah 2:22
   - ☐ Jeremiah 48:7
   - ☐ 1 Corinthians 2:5
   - ☐ 2 Corinthians 1:9
   - ☐ 1 Timothy 6:17

2. **DO NOT TRUST GOD ENOUGH**
   - ☐ Numbers 20:12
   - ☐ Deuteronomy 32:51
   - ☐ Matthew 17:20
   - ☐ Luke 1:20

NOTES

3. DO NOT WAVER IN TOTAL TRUST TO GOD
- ☐ 2 Chronicles 14:11
- ☐ Psalm 26:1
- ☐ Psalm 125:1
- ☐ Proverbs 3:5-6
- ☐ Nahum 1:7
- ☐ Romans 4:20
- ☐ Hebrews 3:14
- ☐ Daniel 6:23

BEFORE YOU PUT THE SHOVEL DOWN
- ☐ Psalm 33:4-10
- ☐ Psalm 37:3-9
- ☐ Psalm 62:8
- ☐ Isaiah 26:3-8
- ☐ Romans 15:13

NOVEMBER 12
The Results of a Holy Audit
Philippians 3:9 (NIV)

1. NOAH WAS FOUND TO BE RIGHTEOUS
- ☐ Genesis 7:1

2. MOSES WAS FOUND WITH FAVOR
- ☐ Exodus 33:12

3. DAVID WAS FOUND TO BE A MAN AFTER GOD'S OWN HEART
- ☐ Acts 13:22

4. BELSHAZZAR WAS FOUND TO BE WANTING
- ☐ Daniel 5:27

5. ABRAHAM WAS FOUND TO BE FAITHFUL
- ☐ Nehemiah 9:7-8

6. CENTURION WAS FOUND TO HAVE GREAT FAITH
- ☐ Luke 7:9

NOVEMBER 13

The Three Dangers of Anxiety

Philippians 4:4-13 (NKJV)

1. **IT CAUSES HARM**
   - ☐ Psalm 37:8

2. **IT CAUSES DEPRESSION**
   - ☐ Proverbs 12:25
   - ☐ Luke 21:34

3. **IT CAUSES INNER TURMOIL**
   - ☐ Job 20:2

NOVEMBER 14

Do Not Be Deceived (NKJV)

- ☐ Genesis 3:13
- ☐ Luke 21:8
- ☐ 1 Corinthians 6:9
- ☐ 1 Corinthians 15:33
- ☐ 2 Corinthians 11:3
- ☐ Galatians 6:7
- ☐ 1 Timothy 2:14
- ☐ 2 Timothy 3:13
- ☐ Titus 3:3
- ☐ James 1:16

NOVEMBER 15

Four Dangerous Kinds of Worship (NLT)

1. **WORSHIP THAT IS FALSE**
   - ☐ Exodus 20:4-5
   - ☐ John 4:24

2. **WORSHIP THAT IS FAKE**
   - ☐ Matthew 15:8-9
   - ☐ Matthew 2:8

3. **WORSHIP THAT FAILS TO BE FAITHFUL**
   - ☐ 1 Kings 11:4

4. **WORSHIP THAT IS OFFERED IN THE FLESH**
   - ☐ Philippians 3:3
   - ☐ John 4:22-23
   - ☐ Acts 17:23

NOVEMBER 16
Seven Things to Cultivate
1 Corinthians 12:31; 14:1 AMP

1. **FAITHFULNESS**
   - ☐ Psalm 37:3 (NASB)

2. **HONEST SPEECH**
   - ☐ Proverbs 16:13 (MSG)

3. **RELATIONSHIP WITH GOD**
   - ☐ Romans 14:22 (MSG)

4. **GOD CONFIDENCE**
   - ☐ 1 Corinthians 10:11 (MSG)

5. **THANKFULNESS**
   - ☐ Colossians 3:15 (MSG)

6. **GOOD**
   - ☐ 1 Peter 3:8 (MSG)

7. **QUIET HEART**
   - ☐ Psalm 131:2 (MSG)

BEFORE YOU PUT THE SHOVEL DOWN
- ☐ 1 Timothy 4:15 (MSG)
- ☐ Philippians 2:12

NOVEMBER 17

Living to Please God: [Part 1]

1 Thessalonians 4:1-3 (NKJV)

God is pleased when:

1. **WE TURN FROM SIN AND TURN TO HIM**
   - ☐ Ezekiel 18:23
   - ☐ Ezekiel 33:11
   - ☐ Psalm 5:4
   - ☐ Luke 15:10

2. **WE USE THE MEASURE OF FAITH HE HAS GIVEN US**
   - ☐ Hebrews 11:6
   - ☐ Hebrews 10:38

3. **WE ARE OBEDIENT TO HIS WORD**
   - ☐ 1 John 3:22
   - ☐ Deuteronomy 12:28 (NLT)
   - ☐ Colossians 3:20

4. **WE WALK WITH HIM DAILY IN DEVOTION**
   - ☐ Hebrews 11:5
   - ☐ Ephesians 5:8-10
   - ☐ Colossians 1:9-10
   - ☐ 1 Chronicles 29:17

5. **WE ARE SPIRITUALLY MINDED NOT EARTHLY FOCUSED**
   - ☐ Romans 8:5-8

6. **WE HAVE A HEALTHY FEAR OF THE LORD**
   - ☐ Psalm 147:10-11

7. **WE IMITATE HIS SON JESUS**
   - ☐ Matthew 3:17; 17:5
   - ☐ 2 Peter 1:17
   - ☐ John 8:29
   - ☐ Ephesians 5:2 (NLT)

8. **WE STRIVE TO ACCOMPLISH HIS WILL**
   - ☐ Hebrews 13:21

NOTES

NOVEMBER 18

Living to Please God: [Part 2] (NKJV)

God is pleased when:

1. **WE DO GOOD FOR OTHERS**
   - ☐ Hebrews 13:15-16
   - ☐ 1 Timothy 5:3-4
   - ☐ Philippians 4:18

2. **WE MEDITATE AND COMMUNICATE HIS THOUGHTS**
   - ☐ Psalm 19:14
   - ☐ Psalm 104:34

3. **WE GIVE HIM PRAISE AND THANKSGIVING**
   - ☐ Psalm 69:30-31

4. **WE CARE MORE ABOUT PLEASING HIM THEN OTHERS**
   - ☐ 1 Thessalonians 2:4
   - ☐ Galatians 1:10

5. **WE PRAY**
   - ☐ 1 Timothy 2:1-3

6. **WE LIVE IN THE POWER OF THE HOLY SPIRIT**
   - ☐ Romans 14:17-18

7. **WE HUMBLE OURSELVES**
   - ☐ Psalm 149:4
   - ☐ Psalm 51:16-17 (NIV)

NOTES

NOVEMBER 19

Four Things You Can Know for Sure About God's Will (NKJV)

It is God's will for you to:

1. **BE SAVED AND HAVE ETERNAL LIFE**
   - ☐ John 6:39-40,47
   - ☐ 2 Peter 3:9

2. **BE UNDER THE INFLUENCE OF THE HOLY SPIRIT**
   - ☐ 1 Thessalonians 4:3,7-8
   - ☐ Ephesians 5:18

3. **GIVE THANKS ALWAYS**
   - ☐ 1 Thessalonians 5:18

4. **DO GOOD**
   - ☐ 1 Peter 2:15; 3:17
   - ☐ Psalm 37:3
   - ☐ Acts 10:38
   - ☐ Matthew 5:16
   - ☐ Galatians 6:9-10

NOVEMBER 20

Things We Are to Always Be Thankful For (NKJV)

- ☐ 2 Corinthians 2:14
- ☐ Ephesians 5:20
- ☐ 1 Thessalonians 1:2
- ☐ 1 Thessalonians 5:18
- ☐ 2 Thessalonians 1:3
- ☐ 2 Thessalonians 2:13

NOVEMBER 21

Always Be (NLT)

1. **EAGER TO SHOW HOSPITALITY**
   - ☐ Romans 12:13

2. **GENEROUS**
   - ☐ 2 Corinthians 9:11

3. **HUMBLE AND GENTLE**
   - ☐ Ephesians 4:2

4. **FILLED WITH THE FRUITS OF YOUR SALVATION**
   - ☐ Philippians 1:11

5. **FULL OF JOY**
   - ☐ Philippians 4:4
   - ☐ 1 Thessalonians 5:16

6. **THANKFUL**
   - ☐ Colossians 3:15

7. **GRACE FILLED IN YOUR SPEECH**
   - ☐ Colossians 4:6 (NKJV)
   - ☐ Ephesians 4:29

8. **READY TO EXPLAIN YOUR HOPE**
   - ☐ 1 Peter 3:15

NOVEMBER 22

The Five Laws of "Thanks-giving:"
[Part 1] *Psalm 100:4 (NLT)*

We are to:

1. **BE THANKFUL AND GIVE THANKS**
   - ☐ Colossians 3:15
   - ☐ Colossians 4:2
   - ☐ Hebrews 12:28
   - ☐ Romans 1:21
   - ☐ 2 Timothy 3:2

2. **GIVE THANKS TO THE LORD**
   - ☐ 1 Chronicles 16:8,34,41
   - ☐ Psalm 92:1
   - ☐ Psalm 105:1
   - ☐ Philippians 4:6 (NKJV)

3. **GIVE THANKS WITH ALL YOUR HEART**
   - ☐ Psalm 138:1
   - ☐ Psalm 9:1
   - ☐ Psalm 86:12
   - ☐ Psalm 111:1

NOVEMBER 23
The Five Laws of "Thanks-giving:"
[Part 2] (NLT)

We are to:

4. **GIVE THANKS CONTINUALLY**
   - ☐ Hebrews 13:15 (NKJV)
   - ☐ Psalm 30:12
   - ☐ Psalm 34:1
   - ☐ Psalm 71:6
   - ☐ Psalm 109:30
   - ☐ Ephesians 5:20

5. **GIVE THANKS IN EVERYTHING**
   - ☐ 1 Thessalonians 5:18
   - ☐ Psalm 34:1

NOVEMBER 24
Seven Observations About Prayer and Missions (NKJV)

1. **PRAYER IS THE CRY OF THE LOST**
   - ☐ Acts 10:31

NOTES

2. **PRAYER FOR GOD'S MISSION ACTIVITY IS THE PURPOSE OF THE CHURCH**
   - ☐ Mark 11:17
   - ☐ Isaiah 56:7
   - ☐ Acts 1:14

3. **PRAYER IS HOW GOD RAISES UP WORKERS FOR THE MISSION FIELD**
   - ☐ Matthew 9:37-38
   - ☐ Luke 10:2
   - ☐ Acts 16:9

4. **PRAYER IS THE VEHICLE THAT OPENS DOORS FOR THE MISSIONARY MESSAGE**
   - ☐ Colossians 4:2-4

5. **PRAYER IS THE FORCE THAT GIVES THE MISSIONARY MESSAGE POWER**
   - ☐ 2 Thessalonians 3:1-2

6. **PRAYER IS THE DESIRE OF EVERY MISSIONARY**
   - ☐ 1 Thessalonians 5:25
   - ☐ Hebrews 13:18

7. **PRAYER IS THE WAY WE CAN STAND IN THE GAP**
   - ☐ Ezekiel 22:30

NOVEMBER 25

10 Things You Must Do *Acts 9:1-6 (NLT)*

1. **YOU MUST BE BORN AGAIN**
   - ☐ John 3:7
   - ☐ Acts 4:12
   - ☐ Acts 16:30

2. **YOU MUST BELIEVE**
   - ☐ Hebrews 11:6
   - ☐ James 1:6 (NIV)

3. **YOU MUST QUICKLY DO THE WORK OF YOUR HEAVENLY FATHER**
   - ☐ John 9:4

4. **YOU MUST DECREASE AND HE MUST INCREASE**
   - ☐ John 3:30

5. **YOU MUST GO THROUGH HARDSHIP**
   - ☐ Acts 14:22
   - ☐ Acts 9:16
   - ☐ 2 Timothy 2:3
   - ☐ Luke 9:22

6. **YOU MUST BE HOLY**
   - ☐ 1 Peter 1:15-16
   - ☐ Romans 6:19

7. **YOU MUST GO INTO ALL THE WORLD**
   - ☐ Mark 13:10
   - ☐ Jeremiah 1:7

8. **YOU MUST GIVE AN ACCOUNT SOMEDAY**
   - ☐ 2 Corinthians 5:10

9. **YOU MUST CONTINUE IN THE THINGS YOU HAVE LEARNED**
   - ☐ 2 Timothy 3:14

10. **YOU MUST FORGIVE OTHERS**
    - ☐ Colossians 3:13

NOVEMBER 26
Four Things the Bible Teaches Us About Grief (NKJV)

1. **GRIEF IS SOMETHING WE WILL ALL FACE IN LIFE**
   - ☐ Ecclesiastes 2:23
   - ☐ Ecclesiastes 3:4

2. CHRIST IS ACQUAINTED WITH OUR GRIEF
- ☐ Isaiah 53:3
- ☐ Matthew 26:38
- ☐ Psalm 10:14
- ☐ Lamentations 3:32

3. GOD'S WORD CAN HELP US THROUGH OUR GRIEF
- ☐ Psalm 119:28
- ☐ Psalm 23
- ☐ Romans 15:4

4. CHRIST CAN HELP TURN YOUR GRIEF INTO JOY
- ☐ John 16:20
- ☐ Jeremiah 31:13

NOVEMBER 27
Five Blessings Associated with Death (NKJV)

1. BLESSED ARE THOSE WHO DIE IN THE LORD
- ☐ Revelation 14:13

2. BLESSED ARE THOSE WHO HAVE LAID UP TREASURES IN HEAVEN
- ☐ Matthew 6:19-20
- ☐ Luke 14:14

3. BLESSED ARE THOSE WHO HAVE THE HOPE OF THE RESURRECTION
- ☐ John 11:25
- ☐ John 5:24
- ☐ 1 Peter 1:3
- ☐ Titus 2:13
- ☐ 1 Thessalonians 4:13
- ☐ Revelation 20:6

4. BLESSED ARE THOSE WHO MOURN, FOR THEY SHALL BE COMFORTED
- ☐ Matthew 5:4
- ☐ 2 Corinthians 1:3-4
- ☐ Psalm 23:4
- ☐ Isaiah 51:12

5. BLESSED ARE THOSE WHO ARE LEFT BEHIND WITH PRECIOUS MEMORIES
- ☐ Proverbs 10:7
- ☐ Psalm 116:15

NOVEMBER 28
Five Reasons Things May Be Happening *Judges 6:1-13 (NIV)*

1. TO FULFILL GOD'S PURPOSE AND PLAN
- ☐ John 15:25 (NKJV)
- ☐ John 19:24
- ☐ Matthew 21:4 (AMP)

2. TO TEACH US TO RELY ON GOD AND NOT OUR SELVES
- ☐ 2 Corinthians 1:9
- ☐ Isaiah 31:1

3. TO ADVANCE THE GOSPEL
- ☐ Matthew 27:54
- ☐ Philippians 1:12-19

4. TO SEE THE POWER OF GOD AT WORK IN OUR LIVES
- ☐ 2 Timothy 3:10-11
- ☐ John 9:3
- ☐ John 11:4,15 (AMP)

5. TO TAKE US ON A DEEPER JOURNEY
- ☐ Galatians 1:13-16 (NLT)

NOTES

NOVEMBER 29

If Someone Sins (NKJV)

1. **GO TO HIM**
   - ☐ Matthew 18:15

2. **REBUKE HIM**
   - ☐ Luke 17:3

3. **FORGIVE HIM**
   - ☐ Luke 17:3-4

4. **RESTORE HIM**
   - ☐ James 5:19-20

NOVEMBER 30

Hope In *Psalm 25:3-21 (NIV)*

Put your hope in:

1. **GOD**
   - ☐ Psalm 42:5,11
   - ☐ Psalm 43:5

2. **GOD'S WORD**
   - ☐ Psalm 119:74,81,114,147
   - ☐ Psalm 130:5

3. **GOD'S UNFAILING LOVE**
   - ☐ Psalm 147:10-11

4. **GOD'S SON JESUS**
   - ☐ Matthew 12:21

NOTES

DECEMBER

DECEMBER 1

The Message of Holiness (NKJV)

1. **YOU NEED TO BE SAVED**
   - ☐ Romans 3:22-23

2. **YOU CAN BE SAVED**
   - ☐ 1 Timothy 2:3-4
   - ☐ Romans 10:12-13

3. **YOU CAN KNOW THEY ARE SAVED**
   - ☐ 1 John 2:3-5
   - ☐ 1 John 3:19-21
   - ☐ 1 John 4:13
   - ☐ 1 John 5:10-13

4. **YOU CAN BE SAVED TO THE UTTERMOST**
   - ☐ Hebrews 7:25

5. **YOU DO NOT HAVE TO CONTINUE IN SIN**
   - ☐ Romans 6:1-22

DECEMBER 2

Three Commands for Christians Regarding the World

2 Corinthians 6:17 (NKJV)

1. **DO NOT LOVE THE WORLD**
   - ☐ 1 John 2:15-16
   - ☐ 2 Timothy 4:10

2. **DO NOT CONFORM TO THE WORLD**
   - ☐ Romans 12:2

3. **DO NOT BE OF THE WORLD**
   - ☐ John 8:23
   - ☐ John 15:18-19
   - ☐ John 17:14-17

DECEMBER 3
Seven Prayers in Times of Trouble
Psalm 20:1-9 (NLT)

1. **MAY THE LORD ANSWER YOUR CRY**
   ☐ Psalm 20:1

2. **MAY THE LORD KEEP YOU SAFE FROM ALL HARM**
   ☐ Psalm 20:1

3. **MAY THE LORD SEND YOU HELP AND STRENGTH**
   ☐ Psalm 20:2

4. **MAY THE LORD REMEMBER YOUR GIFTS AND OFFERINGS**
   ☐ Psalm 20:3

5. **MAY THE LORD GRANT YOUR HEARTS DESIRES AND MAKE YOUR PLANS SUCCEED**
   ☐ Psalm 20:4

6. **MAY OTHERS REJOICE WHEN THEY HEAR OF YOUR VICTORY**
   ☐ Psalm 20:5

7. **MAY THE LORD ANSWER ALL YOUR PRAYERS**
   ☐ Psalm 20:5

NOTES

DECEMBER 4

The Sin of Prayerlessness (NKJV)

Prayerlessness is a sin because:

1. **JESUS COMMANDS HIS FOLLOWERS TO PRAY CONTINUALLY**
   - ☐ Luke 18:1
   - ☐ Romans 12:12
   - ☐ 1 Thessalonians 5:17
   - ☐ Ephesians 6:18
   - ☐ Philippians 4:6
   - ☐ Colossians 4:2

2. **KNOWING WHAT TO DO AND NOT DOING IT IS SIN**
   - ☐ James 4:17

3. **WHEN JESUS DISCIPLES DIDN'T FOLLOW HIS COMMAND TO PRAY, THEY FELL INTO TEMPTATION**
   - ☐ Matthew 26:41
   - ☐ When we don't pray, we fall prey to temptation.

4. **PRAYERLESSNESS IS PRODUCED BY PRIDEFULNESS**
   - ☐ Psalm 10:4
   - ☐ Proverbs 21:4

5. **THE BIBLE CALLS IT A SIN**
   - ☐ 1 Samuel 12:23
   - ☐ Isaiah 30:1-2

6. **WHATEVER WE ASK IN FAITH WE RECEIVE**
   - ☐ Matthew 21:22

7. **WHEN WE DON'T ASK IN FAITH WE SIN**
   - ☐ Romans 14:23

THE SOLUTION TO PRAYERLESSNESS IS TO CONFESS, REPENT AND START TO PRACTICE
   - ☐ James 5:13-18

DECEMBER 5
The Four "Be Still" Commands
Psalm 46 (NIV)

1. **BE STILL AND KNOW**
   - ☐ Psalm 46:10
   - ☐ Psalm 100:3

2. **BE STILL AND WAIT PATIENTLY**
   - ☐ Psalm 37:7

3. **BE STILL AND MEDITATE**
   - ☐ Psalm 4:4

4. **BE STILL AND PRAISE**
   - ☐ Psalm 84:4 (KJV)

BEFORE YOU PUT THE SHOVEL DOWN
- ☐ Zechariah 2:13
- ☐ Exodus 14:13-14 (NKJV)
- ☐ 1 Samuel 12:16
- ☐ Psalm 107:28-29
- ☐ Nehemiah 8:11

DECEMBER 6
Five Weapons When You Face the Enemy
Matthew 4:1-11 (NKJV)

1. **THE HOLY SPIRIT**
   - ☐ Matthew 4:1
   - ☐ Luke 4:1

2. **PRAYER AND FASTING**
   - ☐ Matthew 4:2

3. **THE SCRIPTURE**
   - ☐ Matthew 4:4,7,10

4. STANDING AND SPEAKING AGAINST
- ☐ Matthew 4:4,10
- ☐ Ephesians 6:13-14

5. RESISTING
- ☐ Matthew 4:10
- ☐ James 4:7
- ☐ 1 Peter 5:9

BEFORE YOU PUT THE SHOVEL DOWN
- ☐ 1 Corinthians 10:13
- ☐ Luke 4:13
- ☐ Ephesians 6:10-20

DECEMBER 7
Do Not Be Ignorant Of (NKJV)
- ☐ Romans 10:3
- ☐ Romans 11:25
- ☐ 1 Corinthians 12:1ff
- ☐ 2 Corinthians 1:8
- ☐ 2 Corinthians 2:11
- ☐ 1 Thessalonians 4:13
- ☐ 2 Timothy 2:23

DECEMBER 8
Six Ways to Help Someone Whose Faith is Weak (NIV)

1. ACCEPT THEM
- ☐ Romans 14:1
- ☐ Romans 15:7

2. BEAR WITH THEM
- ☐ Romans 15:1
- ☐ Ephesians 4:2
- ☐ Colossians 3:13

3. BE CAREFUL WITH THEM
- [ ] 1 Corinthians 8:9-12

4. CONNECT WITH THEM
- [ ] 1 Corinthians 9:22

5. HELP THEM
- [ ] 1 Thessalonians 5:14
- [ ] Acts 20:35

6. TEACH THEM
- [ ] Romans 6:19

DECEMBER 9
Seven Unclaimed Blessings for Many Believers (NKJV)

1. BLESSED IS THE MAN WHO WALKS NOT IN THE COUNSEL OF THE UNGODLY
- [ ] Psalm 1:1-2

2. BLESSED IS THE MAN TO WHOM THE LORD DOES NOT IMPUTE INIQUITY
- [ ] Psalm 32:2

3. BLESSED IS THE MAN WHO TRUSTS IN HIM
- [ ] Psalm 34:8
- [ ] Psalm 40:4
- [ ] Psalm 84:12
- [ ] Jeremiah 17:7

4. BLESSED IS THE MAN WHOSE STRENGTH IS IN THE LORD
- [ ] Psalm 84:5

5. BLESSED IS THE MAN WHOM YOU INSTRUCT, O LORD
- [ ] Psalm 94:12
- [ ] Proverbs 8:34

6. **BLESSED IS THE MAN WHO FEARS THE LORD**
   ☐ Psalm 112:1

7. **BLESSED IS THE MAN WHO ENDURES TEMPTATION**
   ☐ James 1:12

DECEMBER 10
The Five Woes in Habakkuk (NKJV)

1. **THE WOE AGAINST AGGRESSION**
   ☐ Habakkuk 2:6-8

2. **THE WOE AGAINST COVETOUSNESS**
   ☐ Habakkuk 2:9-11

3. **THE WOE AGAINST VIOLENCE**
   ☐ Habakkuk 2:12-14

4. **THE WOE AGAINST INHUMANITY**
   ☐ Habakkuk 2:15-17

5. **THE WOE AGAINST IDOLATRY**
   ☐ Habakkuk 2:18-20

DECEMBER 11

The Job Specifications of a Christian *Romans 1:5-7 (NLT)*

Notice the four things, "So that they may:"

1. **BELIEVE**
   - ☐ Romans 1:5a
   - ☐ Mark 1:15
   - ☐ Mark 16:16
   - ☐ John 1:12
   - ☐ John 3:15-18
   - ☐ John 4:39
   - ☐ Romans 3:22,25

2. **OBEY**
   - ☐ Romans 1:5b
   - ☐ Isaiah 1:18-20

3. **BRING GLORY TO HIS NAME**
   - ☐ Romans 1:5c

4. **BELONG**
   - ☐ Romans 1:6

DECEMBER 12

The Birth of John the Baptist
Luke 1:14-80 (NLT)

They rejoiced because:

1. **A PROPHECY HAD BEEN FULFILLED**
   - ☐ Malachi 3:1

2. **A PRAYER HAD BEEN HEARD**
   - ☐ Luke 1:13

3. **A PROMISE HAD BEEN KEPT**
   - ☐ Luke 1:70-73

4. **A PLAN HAD BEEN BIRTHED**
   - ☐ Luke 1:77-79

5. **A PRESENCE HAD BEEN WITNESSED**
   - ☐ Luke 1:15-17; 41-67

DECEMBER 13
Four Different Places in the Scripture That Refer to Christ as the "Prince" [NKJV]

1. **HE IS THE PRINCE OF PRINCES**
   - ☐ Daniel 8:25 (NLT)

2. **HE IS THE PRINCE OF LIFE**
   - ☐ Acts 3:15

3. **HE IS THE PRINCE OF PEACE**
   - ☐ Isaiah 9:6

4. **HE IS THE PRINCE AND SAVIOR**
   - ☐ Acts 5:31

DECEMBER 14
16 Prophecies Fulfilled in the Christmas Story: [Part 1] [NKJV]

1. **GOD'S SON WOULD BE BORN OF A WOMAN**
   - ☐ Genesis 3:15
   - ☐ Galatians 4:4
   - ☐ Luke 2:6-7

2. **HE WOULD BE FROM THE LINE OF ABRAHAM**
   - ☐ Genesis 12:3-7
   - ☐ Genesis 17:7
   - ☐ Matthew 1:1
   - ☐ Romans 9:5
   - ☐ Galatians 3:16

3. **HE WOULD BE FROM THE TRIBE OF JUDAH**
   - ☐ Genesis 49:10
   - ☐ Luke 3:33
   - ☐ Hebrews 7:14
   - ☐ Revelation 5:5

4. **HE WOULD BE FROM THE HOUSE OF DAVID**
   - ☐ 2 Samuel 7:12-13
   - ☐ Psalm 89:3-4
   - ☐ Jeremiah 23:5
   - ☐ Luke 1:31-33; 2:4
   - ☐ Romans 1:3

5. **THERE WOULD BE NO ROOM FOR HIM IN THE INN**
   - ☐ Isaiah 1:3
   - ☐ Luke 2:7

6. **HE WOULD BE BORN OF A VIRGIN**
   - ☐ Isaiah 7:14
   - ☐ Matthew 1:18-23

7. **HE WOULD BE GIVEN THE THRONE OF DAVID**
   - ☐ 2 Samuel 7:11-12
   - ☐ Psalm 132:11
   - ☐ Isaiah 9:6-7
   - ☐ Isaiah 16:5
   - ☐ Jeremiah 23:5
   - ☐ Luke 1:31-32

8. **HIS THRONE WOULD BE AN ETERNAL THRONE**
   - ☐ Daniel 2:44
   - ☐ Daniel 7:14-27
   - ☐ Micah 4:7
   - ☐ Luke 1:33

NOTES

DECEMBER 15

16 Prophecies Fulfilled in the Christmas Story: [Part 2] (NKJV)

9. A TAX WOULD BE IMPOSED AT HIS BIRTH
- ☐ Daniel 11:20
- ☐ Luke 2:3-6

10. HIS NAME WOULD BE EMMANUEL
- ☐ Isaiah 7:14
- ☐ Matthew 1:23

11. HE WOULD HAVE A FORERUNNER
- ☐ Isaiah 40:3-5
- ☐ Malachi 3:1
- ☐ Matthew 3:1-3
- ☐ Luke 1:17,76-78
- ☐ Luke 3:3-6

12. HE WOULD BE BORN IN BETHLEHEM
- ☐ Micah 5:2
- ☐ Matthew 2:5-6
- ☐ Luke 2:4-6

13. HE WOULD BE WORSHIPPED BY WISE MEN AND PRESENTED WITH GIFTS
- ☐ Psalm 72:10
- ☐ Isaiah 60:3-9
- ☐ Matthew 2:11

14. HE WOULD BE IN EGYPT FOR A SEASON
- ☐ Numbers 24:8
- ☐ Hosea 11:1
- ☐ Matthew 2:14-15

15. HIS BIRTHPLACE WOULD SUFFER A MASSACRE OF INFANTS
- ☐ Jeremiah 31:15
- ☐ Matthew 2:16-18

16. HE WOULD BE CALLED A NAZARENE
- ☐ Isaiah 11:1
- ☐ Isaiah 53:2
- ☐ Matthew 2:23

DECEMBER 16

Six Benefits of Taking the Time to Think About Things *Matthew 1:19-24 (NKJV)*

1. **YOU GIVE GOD A CHANCE TO SPEAK**
   ☐ Matthew 1:20

2. **YOU ARE ABLE TO GET THE FACTS**
   ☐ Matthew 1:20b

3. **YOU ARE ABLE TO CHANGE YOUR MIND IF NECESSARY**
   ☐ Matthew 1:19-20

4. **YOU ARE ABLE TO ASSEMBLE A GOD PLAN INSTEAD OF YOUR OWN GAME PLAN**
   ☐ Matthew 1:24

5. **YOU ARE ABLE TO FIND PEACE IN THE MIDST OF YOUR PROBLEM**
   ☐ Matthew 1:20

6. **YOU ARE ABLE TO BE APART OF SOMETHING GOD IS DOING**
   ☐ Matthew 1:24-25

DECEMBER 17

Seven Keys to Being Used by God
Luke 1 (NKJV)

God is looking for:

1. **A LIFESTYLE THAT HONORS GOD**
   ☐ Luke 1:28,30

2. **A WALK THROUGH THE IMPOSSIBLE**
   ☐ Luke 1:27

3. **A WILLINGNESS TO UNCONDITIONALLY ACCEPT THE CALL OF GOD IN YOUR LIFE**
   ☐ Luke 1:38

4. **A FRESH FILLING OF THE HOLY SPIRIT**
   ☐ Luke 1:35

5. **AN OVERSHADOWING OF THE POWER OF GOD IN YOUR LIFE**
   ☐ Luke 1:35

6. **A HEART THAT TREASURES THE WAYS OF GOD**
   ☐ Luke 2:18-19 (NIV)

7. **A COMMITMENT TO CARRY OUT THE ROLE YOU WERE CALLED TO PLAY**
   ☐ Luke 2:20-24

DECEMBER 18
The "Fear Nots" of Christmas (KJV)

Several "fear nots" are included in the Christmas narratives:

1. **THE "FEAR NOT" OF SALVATION**
   ☐ Luke 2:10,11

2. **THE "FEAR NOT" OF THE HUMANLY IMPOSSIBLE**
   ☐ Luke 1:30,35,37

3. **THE "FEAR NOT" OF UNANSWERED PRAYER**
   ☐ Luke 1:13

4. **THE "FEAR NOT" OF IMMEDIATE OBEDIENCE**
   ☐ Matthew 1:20,24

DECEMBER 19

The Christmas Story Where You Least Expect to Find It: [Part 1] (NKJV)

- [ ] Job 9:33 (NLT)
- [ ] Isaiah 7:14
- [ ] Isaiah 9:6
- [ ] Micah 5:2
- [ ] Zechariah 9:9
- [ ] Luke 19:10
- [ ] John 1:9-14
- [ ] John 3:16

DECEMBER 20

The Christmas Story Where You Least Expect to Find It: [Part 2] (NKJV)

- [ ] John 10:10
- [ ] John 18:37
- [ ] 2 Corinthians 8:9
- [ ] 2 Corinthians 9:15
- [ ] Galatians 4:4-5
- [ ] Philippians 2:5-11

DECEMBER 21

The Christmas Story Where You Least Expect to Find It: [Part 3] (NKJV)

- [ ] Colossians 1:15-20
- [ ] 1 Timothy 1:15
- [ ] Titus 3:4-6
- [ ] James 1:17
- [ ] Hebrews 2:9
- [ ] Revelation 12:5

NOTES

DECEMBER 22
The Glory of Christmas John 1:14 (NKJV)

1. **JESUS CAME IN GLORY**
   - ☐ Luke 2:9
2. **JESUS LIVED IN GLORY**
   - ☐ John 1:14
3. **JESUS WILL RETURN IN GLORY**
   - ☐ Matthew 24:30

DECEMBER 23
His Name Shall Be Called Prince of Peace Isaiah 9:6-7 (NKJV)

Because Jesus is the Prince of Peace, it is possible to have peace:

1. **WITH GOD**
   - ☐ Romans 5:1
   - ☐ Romans 8:6
   - ☐ Ephesians 2:14-17
2. **FROM YOUR SHAMEFUL PAST**
   - ☐ Luke 7:36-50
3. **THROUGH SICKNESS AND SUFFERING**
   - ☐ Mark 5:34
   - ☐ Luke 8:48
4. **IN THE MIDST OF THE STORMS OF LIFE**
   - ☐ Mark 4:39
5. **FROM BROKEN RELATIONSHIPS**
   - ☐ Romans 12:18
   - ☐ Matthew 5:9
   - ☐ Romans 14:19
   - ☐ 2 Corinthians 13:11
   - ☐ Mark 9:50

NOTES

6. **IN THE MIDST OF UNCERTAINTY**
   - ☐ Luke 24:36
   - ☐ John 20:19,21,26

7. **WHILE WE BATTLE WITH THE ENEMY**
   - ☐ Romans 16:20
   - ☐ John 16:33

DECEMBER 24
16 Reasons Why Jesus Came: [Part 1] (NKJV)

1. **BE A LIGHT TO THE WORLD**
   - ☐ John 12:46

2. **SEEK AND SAVE THE LOST**
   - ☐ Luke 19:10
   - ☐ Luke 9:56
   - ☐ John 3:17
   - ☐ Mark 2:17
   - ☐ 1 Timothy 1:15

3. **GIVE HIS LIFE FOR A RANSOM**
   - ☐ Matthew 20:28
   - ☐ Hebrews 9:26-28
   - ☐ John 12:27

4. **DO GOD'S WILL**
   - ☐ John 6:38

5. **FULFILL THE LAW AND THE PROPHETS**
   - ☐ Matthew 5:17

6. **DESTROY THE WORKS OF THE DEVIL**
   - ☐ 1 John 3:8
   - ☐ Hebrews 2:14
   - ☐ Colossians 2:15

7. **SERVE**
   - ☐ Mark 10:45

8. **REVEAL GOD TO US**
   - ☐ John 1:14
   - ☐ Matthew 11:27

DECEMBER 25

16 Reasons Why Jesus Came: [Part 2] [NKJV]

9. CARRY OUR BURDENS
- ☐ Matthew 11:28
- ☐ 1 Peter 5:6-7

10. MEDIATE BETWEEN GOD AND MAN
- ☐ 1 Timothy 2:5
- ☐ Hebrews 8:6
- ☐ Hebrews 12:24

11. GIVE US ABUNDANT LIFE
- ☐ John 10:10

12. BRING JUDGMENT
- ☐ John 9:39
- ☐ Luke 12:49

13. DIVIDE
- ☐ Luke 12:51
- ☐ Matthew 25:32

14. PREACH THE KINGDOM OF GOD
- ☐ Luke 4:43
- ☐ Mark 1:38

15. BEAR WITNESS TO THE TRUTH
- ☐ John 18:37

16. SET THE CAPTIVES FREE
- ☐ Luke 4:18

DECEMBER 26
Seven Good Qualities of a Godly Mother *Luke 1-2 (NLT)*

1. **MARY HAD A CONSISTENT WALK WITH THE LORD**
   - ☐ Luke 1:28

2. **MARY WAS ATTENTIVE TO GOD'S WORD**
   - ☐ Luke 1:31-38

3. **MARY CARRIED OUT GOD'S PLAN TO FULL TERM**
   - ☐ Luke 1:39-45

4. **MARY EXPRESSED HER WORSHIP IN A SPIRIT OF HUMILITY**
   - ☐ Luke 1:46-55

5. **MARY QUICKLY ADAPTED TO GOD'S UNEXPECTED CHANGES**
   - ☐ Luke 2:3,7

6. **MARY PONDERED THE THINGS OF GOD IN HER HEART**
   - ☐ Luke 2:19

7. **MARY LAVISHLY LOVED DESPITE THE POSSIBILITY HER HEART WOULD BE PIERCED**
   - ☐ Luke 2:35

NOTES

DECEMBER 27
Four Things You Need to Know [NKJV]

1. **GOD IS FOR US**
   - ☐ Romans 8:31
   - ☐ Psalm 124:1

2. **GOD IS WITH US**
   - ☐ Matthew 1:23
   - ☐ Acts 7:9
   - ☐ Matthew 28:20

3. **GOD DESIRES TO BE IN US**
   - ☐ Colossians 1:27
   - ☐ Revelation 3:20
   - ☐ 1 John 3:24
   - ☐ Ephesians 3:17
   - ☐ Romans 8:11

4. **GOD WANTS TO WORK THROUGH US**
   - ☐ 2 Corinthians 2:14

DECEMBER 28
The Five Excuses Moses Made
Exodus 3-4 (NKJV)

1. **WHO AM I THAT I SHOULD GO?**
   - ☐ Exodus 3:11

2. **WHAT SHALL I SAY TO THEM?**
   - ☐ Exodus 3:13-14

3. **WHAT IF THEY DO NOT LISTEN TO ME?**
   - ☐ Exodus 4:1

4. **I AM NOT ELOQUENT AND CANNOT SPEAK WELL**
   ☐ Exodus 4:10

5. **LORD, IF YOU DON'T MIND JUST SEND SOMEONE ELSE**
   ☐ Exodus 4:13

DECEMBER 29
Get Rid Of (NLT)

1. **YOUR IDOLS**
   ☐ Genesis 35:2
   ☐ 1 Samuel 7:3

2. **YOUR VILE IMAGES**
   ☐ Ezekiel 20:7-8

3. **THE LOG IN YOUR OWN EYE**
   ☐ Matthew 7:4-5
   ☐ Luke 6:42

4. **THE OLD YEAST**
   ☐ 1 Corinthians 5:6-7
   ☐ Matthew 16:6,11-12

5. **YOUR SINFUL BEHAVIOR**
   ☐ Ephesians 4:30-32
   ☐ Colossians 3:5-11

6. **ALL EVIL AND FILTH**
   ☐ James 1:19-21
   ☐ 1 Peter 2:1-3

DECEMBER 30
The "You Musts" of Peter (NLT)

You must:

1. **ENDURE TRIALS**
   ☐ 1 Peter 1:6

2. **LIVE AS GOD'S OBEDIENT CHILDREN**
   ☐ 1 Peter 1:14

3. **BE HOLY**
   ☐ 1 Peter 1:15

4. **LIVE IN REVERENT FEAR**
   ☐ 1 Peter 1:17

5. **SHOW SINCERE LOVE TO EACH OTHER**
   ☐ 1 Peter 1:22

6. **CRAVE PURE SPIRITUAL MILK**
   ☐ 1 Peter 2:2

7. **FOLLOW IN HIS FOOTSTEPS**
   ☐ 1 Peter 2:21

8. **WORSHIP CHRIST**
   ☐ 1 Peter 3:15

9. **ARM YOURSELF AND BE READY**
   ☐ 1 Peter 4:1

10. **PAY CLOSE ATTENTION**
    ☐ 2 Peter 1:19

11. **UNDERSTAND THE ORIGIN OF SCRIPTURE**
    ☐ 2 Peter 1:20

12. **NOT FORGET**
    ☐ 2 Peter 3:8

13. **GROW IN GRACE**
    ☐ 2 Peter 3:18

NOTES

DECEMBER 31
Paul's Prayers of Benediction (NLT)

- [ ] Romans 15:5-6,13,33
- [ ] 2 Corinthians 13:14
- [ ] Ephesians 3:16-19
- [ ] Philippians 1:9-11
- [ ] Colossians 1:9-11
- [ ] 1 Thessalonians 3:11-13
- [ ] 1 Thessalonians 5:23-24
- [ ] 2 Thessalonians 2:16-17
- [ ] 2 Thessalonians 3:5,16
- [ ] Hebrews 13:20-21

NOTES

ACKNOWLEDGMENTS

I want to thank my brother Rev. Ray Jones for serving as the Scripture editor of this book. Thanks, Ray, for making sure every reference in this book is accurate. I appreciate your dedication to details for this devotional.

I want to thank our publishing team from Christian Medical & Dental Associations (CMDA) for producing this devotional book. Special thanks to Barbara Snapp, Publishing Manager; to Mandi Morrin, who serves as Vice President of Communication and Events and edited the book; and to Dina Sorn, who served as the designer for this project.

I would also like to thank CMDA CEO Dr. Mike Chupp, who continued to ask me in our weekly one-on-one meetings, "What's the next book you are working on?" Your question encouraged me to complete this discipleship devotional.

I would also like to give a special shoutout to my wife Cheryl, who I typically share every sermon idea with before I preach it. She heard most of these outlines in their infant stage and gave me her input and encouragement. She also sat in the audience and heard a number of these messages live. Thanks for your prayers, encouragements and suggestions over the years that improved these messages.

TOPICAL INDEX

JANUARY
1. Five Sin Problems That Cause Us Trouble 18
2. Where We Can Find Encouragement 19
3. Symbols of the Spirit: [Part 1] 19
4. Symbols of the Spirit: [Part 2] 20
5. Three Kinds of Peace 21
6. Three People Who Ask One Question 21
7. The Three Prayers for Revival 22
8. The Three Levels of Evil 22
9. The Second Coming: [Part 1] 23
10. The Second Coming: [Part 2] 24
11. The Purpose Statements of Jesus: [Part 1] 25
12. The Purpose Statements of Jesus: [Part 2] 26
13. The Purpose Statements of Jesus: [Part 3] 27
14. Suggestions for Serving the Lord 27
15. Living to Please God: [Part 1] 28
16. Living to Please God: [Part 2] 29
17. Living to Please God: [Part 3] 29
18. Commands for Spirit-filled Living 30
19. Three Common Ways We Commit Sin 31
20. Five Ways to Overcome the Devil 31
21. Five Things You Need to Know About God's Gift of Salvation 32
22. Seven Things God Does With Sin 32
23. Seven Things You Cannot Live Without 33
24. Eight Things We Should Do With Sin 34
25. Six Warnings Regarding the Holy Spirit 35
26. Five Keys to Being Justified 36
27. God's Desire 36
28. Whoever 37
29. The "I Am" Statements of Jesus in John 38
30. Five Responsibilities We Have Toward Those in Authority 38
31. The Holy Spirit is Given to Those Who 40

FEBRUARY
1. Trust Him Even When 42
2. The Three Types of Godliness 42
3. God Is Able To 43
4. Satan's Strategy 44
5. Three Examples of Forgiveness 44
6. Bless the Lord 45
7. Unless 46
8. Four Areas God Will Judge You 46
9. Three Levels of Righteousness 47
10. Three Things I Must Do Today 47
11. Four Things You Should Continually Commit to the Lord 48
12. Biblical Aid When My Heart is Afraid 49
13. Seven Dangerous Love Affairs in Scripture 50
14. Three "Let Us Love" Passages 51
15. Four Things You Should Do Quickly 51
16. Grace Does Not Erase the Need for Good Deeds 52
17. The New Testament "Walk" Commandments 53
18. The Four-fold Purpose for Why Jesus Was Manifested 54
19. The 15 Things "We Know" in 1 John 54
20. Five Things God Requires of Us 55
21. Are You the One? 55
22. The Battle 56
23. Six Giving Requirements 57
24. I Am Resolved 58
25. The Five Problems of Not Inquiring of the Lord 58
26. Three Practices of Jesus That Could Change Your Life 59
27. Elements of a Quality Quiet Time 59
28. The Secret to Seeking God 61
29. Eight Things the Bible Challenges Us to Do Wholeheartedly 62

MARCH
1. What the Bible Has to Say About Itself 66
2. 11 Paradoxes in the New Testament: [Part 1] 67
3. 11 Paradoxes in the New Testament: [Part 2] 68
4. Four Proofs We Are Still Controlled By the Sinful Nature 68
5. When Making a Decision 69
6. What Does It Profit? 70
7. Satan and His Schemes: [Part 1] 71
8. Satan and His Schemes: [Part 2] 72
9. The Three Dangers of Anxiety 73
10. Seven Ways God May Use a Test 73
11. Four Keys to Spiritual Growth 74
12. Be of Good Cheer 75
13. Three Conclusions About Comfort 75
14. Comfort Comes From 76

15. Three Critical Turns in Life's Journey 77
16. Three Dangerous Turns Once You've Turned to God 77
17. Three Inappropriate Approaches to Sin 78
18. The Three Little Bears in Scripture 78
19. Three Keys to Prayer 79
20. Five Things the Bible Tells Us to Flee From 79
21. Three Commands for Christians Regarding the World 80
22. Four Things the Bible Teaches We Must Work At 80
23. Who Then Can Be Saved? 81
24. Three Times God's Voice Was Heard Regarding His Son 82
25. The End of the World is Coming Soon Therefore 82
26. Let Us 83
27. We Are to Acknowledge 84
28. The Autopsy of Sin 85
29. The Plot to Kill Jesus: [Part 1] 86
30. The Plot to Kill Jesus: [Part 2] 87
31. Six Dangerous Things to Refuse 88

APRIL

1. Five Types of Fools in Scripture 90
2. Four Things We Are Commanded to Do Without Doubting 90
3. Seven Things God Doesn't Know 91
4. Seven Things We Must Learn 92
5. The Three Crosses at Calvary 93
6. The Proof of Our Salvation in 1 John 94
7. The Seven Last Words of Jesus on the Cross 95
8. The Seven Kinds of People God Will Not Save 95
9. The Seven Things God Requires of You 96
10. Signs of the Second Coming 97
11. Seven Things God Does Not Want You to Forget 98
12. The Four Blessings of Going 99
13. Four Ways to Overcome 99
14. Four Things That Helped Jesus Through His Time of Temptation 100
15. God is Attentive to These Prayers 100
16. The Greatest Question of All: "What Shall We Do?" 101
17. One Thing 101
18. Four Things to Do Continually 102
19. Five Benefits of the Blood of Christ 102
20. God Positions Himself 103
21. The Six Great Commission Passages 104
22. A Christian Should 104
23. The Importance of Faith 105
24. But Let 105
25. The Three Back Conditions in Scripture 106
26. The Blessed Hope 106
27. The Four "Alls" of Blessing 107
28. The Three Times Jesus Wept 107
29. Four-part Harmony 108
30. Paul's Five Great Fears 108

MAY

1. Two Helps Toward Holiness 110
2. The Measure You Use Will Be Measured to You 110
3. Definitions of Sin 110
4. 10 Things That Glorify God: [Part 1] 111
5. 10 Things That Glorify God: [Part 2] 112
6. Old Testament Beatitudes: [Part 1] 112
7. Old Testament Beatitudes: [Part 2] 113
8. The Truth About Lying: [Part 1] 114
9. The Truth About Lying: [Part 2] 115
10. Bad Things You Can Be Filled With 116
11. Six Things the Bible Teaches Us About Light 116
12. Five Truths About Darkness 117
13. Five Things We Are Commanded to Put On 118
14. Six "Be" Commands in Ephesians 118
15. The Seven Gifts of Christ 119
16. Seven Observations About Thorns in the Bible 119
17. Six Things God Desires More Than Sacrifice 120
18. Six Spiritual Priorities You Can't Afford to Neglect 121
19. Divine Discipline 122
20. You're Only Fooling Yourself When 123
21. Is Anything Too Hard for the Lord? 124
22. The Answers for Unanswered Prayer 124
23. The God Who Sees 126
24. What Does It Profit? 126
25. Life in Christ 127
26. A Simple Prayer 127
27. Two Kinds of Appearance to Avoid 128
28. Six Reasons Not to Judge 128
29. To Enjoy Life and See Many Happy Days 129
30. The Carnality of Partiality 129
31. Three Dangers in Our Spiritual Journey 130

JUNE

1. God is the Author Of 132
2. Three Temperatures of the Heart 132
3. You Cannot...Unless 132
4. The Basics of Being Born Again 133
5. Five Good Things That Will Not Get You to Heaven 134
6. The Marks of a Great Church 134
7. The Unfavorable Nature of Favoritism 135
8. The Six Sins of Sodom and Gomorrah 136
9. The Benefits to Those Who Fear God 137
10. The Tongue 137
11. Regarding the Righteous 138
12. Seven Things the Godly Will Follow After 139
13. The Eight Things God Hates 139
14. What It Means to Follow Christ: [Part 1] 140
15. What It Means to Follow Christ: [Part 2] 141

16. The Marks of True Greatness 142
17. Stop Signs in Scripture: [Part 1] 143
18. Stop Signs in Scripture: [Part 2] 143
19. The "Above Alls" in Scripture 144
20. Two Spiritual Threats 144
21. Seven Marks of Spiritually Mature Christians 144
22. Paul's 10 Commandments for Living in a Crooked and
    Perverse Generation 146
23. The Benefits of Belonging to Christ 147
24. The Secret of Contentment 148
25. The Fruit of Righteousness: [Part 1] 149
26. The Fruit of Righteousness: [Part 2] 150
27. The Carnal Mind Versus the Mind of Christ 151
28. Seven Reasons Abiding is Absolutely Essential 153
29. Four Negative Reactions to the Resurrection 154
30. What to Do When Everything is Falling Apart 154

JULY

1. Three Commands for Christians Regarding the World 156
2. Ananias and Sapphira 156
3. The Works of the Lord 157
4. Your Freedom 158
5. Polluted Christian Living 158
6. Four Stages of Spiritual Growth 159
7. Five Invitations of Christ 159
8. The Cost of Calvary 160
9. Two Ways of Life 161
10. Two Kinds of Death 161
11. 10 Descriptions of the Wicked 162
12. Our Relationship With Christ 163
13. God's Grace 163
14. Paul's Five Key "I" Statements in Philippians 164
15. Seven Biblical Practices Great Leaders Follow 164
16. God's Word on Not Giving Up 165
17. Five Things We Are to Make Every Effort 166
18. Those Who Will Find Themselves in the Lake of Fire 166
19. The Secret to Staying Strong in Life's Struggles 167
20. Six Observations About Sanctification 168
21. Holiness 169
22. Three Things Must Happen in the Life of Every Disciple 170
23. Everyone Involved in Missions 170
24. If You Do This 171
25. God is Attracted to Weakness 172
26. Postures of Prayer in the Bible 172
27. Three Responses to the Devil 174
28. Powerful Prayers 174
29. The Seven Excepts in the Bible 175
30. The Four Things God Does After You Suffer Awhile 175
31. Six Basic Beliefs 176

AUGUST

1. It's Worth Repeating, "Love Your Neighbor as Yourself" 180
2. Four Important Words in Your Spiritual Journey 180
3. Do Everything 181
4. The Seven Blessings Revealed in Revelation 181
5. What Does the Bible Have to Say About Marriage? 182
6. Four Things to Stir Up 182
7. Seven Ways We Should Live As 183
8. May I Never Forget 183
9. Four Things Pride Leads To 184
10. Prescription for Spiritual Victory 184
11. The Lord is Close 185
12. Note Those 185
13. Biblical Instruction for Husbands 186
14. Biblical Instruction for Wives 186
15. What the Bible Teaches About Sex Before Marriage 187
16. What the Bible Teaches About Sex After Marriage 188
17. Those Who Will Not Inherit the Kingdom of God 188
18. Five Things the Bible Has to Say About Anger 189
19. "If We Say" Statements 190
20. The "If . . . Then" Clauses 190
21. What the Bible Has to Say About Fellowship 191
22. Biblical Definitions of Sin 191
23. Five Responsibilities Toward Those We See Sinning 192
24. The 21 Works of The Devil: [Part 1] 193
25. The 21 Works of The Devil: [Part 2] 194
26. The Five Old Testament Covenants 195
27. Six Stewardship Laws 195
28. The Eight Causes of Financial Bondage 196
29. What the Lord Knows About the Righteous 197
30. Watch What You Practice 197
31. The "As For Me" Passages 198

SEPTEMBER

1. The Message of Missions in the Book of Psalms 200
2. The Impact of Every 200
3. Your Faith Can Change the World 201
4. Personal Instructions: [Part 1] 201
5. Personal Instructions: [Part 2] 202
6. The 10 "Stand" Commands in Scripture: [Part 1] 203
7. The 10 Stand Commands in Scripture: [Part 2] 203
8. Four Simple Commands 204
9. David's Favorite Prayer, "Have Mercy on Me" 205
10. Six Acts That Can Change the World 205
11. The Upheaval of Evil 206
12. See To It 207
13. God Of 208
14. When You Face the Uncertainty of Difficulty: [Part 1] 208
15. When You Face the Uncertainty of Difficulty: [Part 2] 209

16. 10 Keys to the Kingdom of Heaven in Matthew 210
17. Seven Marks of a Disciple 211
18. Beginning of Life Scriptures 212
19. Seven Truths About Temptation 213
20. How to Overcome Temptation 213
21. Six Things We Can Learn About Prayer from the Garden 214
22. The Biblical Basis for Reaching the Lost 215
23. Jesus' Approach to Lost People 216
24. God Loves Us Even When 217
25. The Maze of God's Ways 218
26. Hidden Sins 219
27. Four Truths About Our Words 220
28. 11 Things the Bible Tells You to Do With All Your Heart 220
29. The Daily Disciplines of a Disciple of Christ 221
30. Prudent Behavior 222

OCTOBER

1. Five Crowns in Scripture 224
2. Six Different Types of Rewards 224
3. There Are Great Rewards in Heaven 225
4. Three Regular Exams We Must Take 226
5. The 15 Attributes of the Pharisees: [Part 1] 227
6. The 15 Attributes of the Pharisees: [Part 2] 228
7. Six Things Jesus Did to Accomplish the Will of God 228
8. Six Present Things God Rescues Us From 230
9. Four Keys to "Whatever We Ask" in Prayer 230
10. Four Contaminating Spirits Within a Congregation 231
11. Some Facts About God's Love 232
12. Don't Be Surprised 233
13. What the Bible Says About Self-control 234
14. Stay Away From 235
15. The Only Two Things That Amazed Jesus 236
16. Standing on the Promises 236
17. You Can Be Sure 237
18. Five Things to Do Without Wavering 238
19. The Lord is My 239
20. The Pledge 240
21. Six Benchmarks of the Born Again 241
22. Serve the Lord 242
23. Beware of Greed 242
24. Paul's Six Charges to Timothy 243
25. What the Bible Teaches About Our Reputation 244
26. The Riches of God 245
27. If We Wait on the Lord 246
28. Waiting Commands 247
29. Seven New Testament Secrets to Living in the Light 247
30. An Abomination to the Lord 248
31. The Word on Witchcraft 248

NOVEMBER

1. The Four "Alls" in the Great Commission 250
2. Six Ways to Pray for the Missions Message 250
3. 10 Duties of a Congregation to Their Pastor: [Part 1] 251
4. 10 Duties of a Congregation to Their Pastor: [Part 2] 252
5. Six Things That Will Help Us Be Strong 252
6. Seven Things Scripture Teaches Us About Persecution: [Part 1] 253
7. Seven Things Scripture Teaches Us About Persecution: [Part 2] 254
8. We Will Give an Account 255
9. Six Common Struggles 256
10. Seven Keys to Justification 256
11. Three Degrees of Trusting God 257
12. The Results of a Holy Audit 258
13. The Three Dangers of Anxiety 259
14. Do Not Be Deceived 259
15. Four Dangerous Kinds of Worship 259
16. Seven Things to Cultivate 260
17. Living to Please God: [Part 1] 261
18. Living to Please God: [Part 2] 262
19. Four Things You Can Know for Sure About God's Will 263
20. Things We Are to Always Be Thankful For 263
21. Always Be 264
22. The Five Laws of "Thanks-giving:" [Part 1] 264
23. The Five Laws of "Thanks-giving:" [Part 2] 265
24. Seven Observations About Prayer and Missions 265
25. 10 Things You Must Do 266
26. Four Things the Bible Teaches Us About Grief 267
27. Five Blessings Associated with Death 268
28. Five Reasons Things May Be Happening 269
29. If Someone Sins 270
30. Hope In 270

DECEMBER

1. The Message of Holiness 272
2. Three Commands for Christians Regarding the World 272
3. Seven Prayers in Times of Trouble 273
4. The Sin of Prayerlessness 274
5. The Four "Be Still" Commands 275
6. Five Weapons When You Face the Enemy 275
7. Do Not Be Ignorant Of 276
8. Six Ways to Help Someone Whose Faith is Weak 276
9. Seven Unclaimed Blessings for Many Believers 277
10. The Five Woes in Habakkuk 278
11. The Job Specifications of a Christian 279
12. The Birth of John the Baptist 279
13. Four Different Places in the Scripture That Refer to Christ as the "Prince" 280
14. 16 Prophecies Fulfilled in the Christmas Story: [Part 1] 280
15. 16 Prophecies Fulfilled in the Christmas Story: [Part 2] 282

16. Six Benefits of Taking the Time to Think About Things 283
17. Seven Keys to Being Used by God 283
18. The "Fear Nots" of Christmas 284
19. The Christmas Story Where You Least Expect to Find It: [Part 1] 285
20. The Christmas Story Where You Least Expect to Find It: [Part 2] 285
21. The Christmas Story Where You Least Expect to Find It: [Part 3] 285
22. The Glory of Christmas 286
23. His Name Shall Be Called Prince of Peace 286
24. 16 Reasons Why Jesus Came: [Part 1] 287
25. 16 Reasons Why Jesus Came: [Part 2] 288
26. Seven Good Qualities of a Godly Mother 289
27. Four Things You Need to Know 290
28. The Five Excuses Moses Made 290
29. Get Rid Of 291
30. The "You Musts" of Peter 292
31. Paul's Prayers of Benediction 293

ABOUT THE AUTHOR
BERT L. JONES, ACC

Pastor Bert serves as Vice President of Missions and Member Care for Christian Medical & Dental Associations (CMDA) in Bristol, Tennessee. In this role, Bert oversees all the mission outreach ministries of CMDA and the Center for Well-Being. Bert also serves as chaplain and coach for CMDA. Bert is a certified ACC coach with the International Coaching Federation. Bert loves coaching healthcare professionals, pastors, ministry leaders, business leaders and missionaries.

Since 1988, Bert has led multiple mission teams across the street and around the world. Bert has traveled on five different continents and to more than 40 different countries to teach and preach the gospel. He is active in leadership development and coaching nationally and internationally. His heart is to coach leaders to discover God's purpose and plan for their lives and reach their God-given potential.

In addition to this book, Bert is the author of *The Leadership Journal from a Leader's Journey*, published by CMDA in 2022. He also co-authored *Servant Leadership* and *Leadership Proverbs* with Dr. David Stevens. In addition, Bert is the author of *Practical Youth Ministry*, published by Bristol Books. Bert frequently writes and teaches on the subject of leadership. Bert is also a certified instructor for the Perspectives in World Missions Course.

Bert holds his ordination through the Missionary Church USA. The Missionary Church is an evangelical denomination committed to church planting and world missions. Bert is under special appointment from the Missionary Church to CMDA. Pastor Bert also serves on the preaching team at South Bristol Church in Bristol, Tennessee when he is not traveling.

Prior to rejoining the staff of CMDA, Bert served as the Senior Pastor of Woodburn Missionary Church from 2014 to 2021 and as the President and CEO of GO International. Bert previously served with CMDA as Chaplain and Director of Leadership and Church Ministries. In 1998, Bert planted Harvest Community Church in Kittanning, Pennsylvania and served as its lead pastor. Bert has served both in the local church and in parachurch organizations throughout his ministry.

Bert graduated from Asbury University in 1989 with a degree in Bible. Bert finished two years of seminary at Pittsburgh Theological Seminary. Bert and his wife Cheryl have been married since 1989 and have three children: Joshua, Allyson and Aaron. His wife Cheryl is a teacher and is active in their ministry. Joshua and his wife Kali have two children, Judah and Oswyn. Bert's favorite title is "Papaw."

Founded in 1931, CMDA provides programs and services supporting its mission to educate, encourage, and equip Christian healthcare professionals to glorify God. Christian healthcare professionals glorify God by following Christ, serving with excellence and compassion, caring for all people, and advancing Biblical principles impacting healthcare within the Church and throughout the world. To learn more about the Christian Medical & Dental Associations, including how to join this movement of Christian healthcare professionals, go to www.cmda.org or call 1-888-230-2637.